Before & After DECORATING

HGTV Before & After Decorating
Editor: Amy Tincher-Durik
Art Director: Chad Owen, Owen Design
Contributing Editor: Paula Marshall
Copy Chief: Terri Fredrickson
Copy and Production Editor: Victoria Forlini
Editorial Operations Manager: Karen Schirm
Managers, Book Production: Pam Kvitne, Marjorie J. Schenkelberg, Rick von Holdt
Contributing Copy Editor: Jane Woychick
Contributing Proofreaders: Sara Henderson, Nancy Ruhling, Margaret Smith
Illustrator: Tom Buchs
Indexer: Elizabeth Parson
Electronic Production Coordinator: Paula Forest
Editorial and Design Assistants: Kaye Chabot, Karen McFadden, Mary Lee Gavin

Meredith® Books
Editor in Chief: Linda Raglan Cunningham
Design Director: Matt Strelecki
Executive Editor, Home Decorating and Design: Denise L. Caringer

Publisher: James D. Blume
Executive Director, Marketing: Jeffrey Myers
Executive Director, New Business Development: Todd M. Davis
Executive Director, Sales: Ken Zagor
Director, Operations: George A. Susral
Director, Production: Douglas M. Johnston
Business Director: Jim Leonard

Vice President and General Manager: Douglas J. Guendel

Meredith Publishing Group
President, Publishing Group: Stephen M. Lacy
Vice President-Publishing Director: Bob Mate

Meredith Corporation
Chairman and Chief Executive Officer: William T. Kerr

In Memoriam E. T. Meredith III (1933-2003)

All of us at Meredith® Books are dedicated to providing you with information and ideas to enhance your home. We welcome your comments and suggestions. Write to us at: Meredith Books, Home Decorating and Design Editorial Department, 1716 Locust St., Des Moines, IA 50309-3023.

If you would like to purchase any of our home decorating and design, cooking, crafts, gardening, or home improvement books, check wherever quality books are sold. Or visit us at: meredithbooks.com

For more information on the topics included in this book as well as additional projects, visit HGTV.com/beforeandafterbook

Cover photograph: Lark Smothermon/Woolly Bugger Studios

Table of Contents

Introduction

Like the programs on HGTV, this book takes the guesswork out of restyling your home. The makeovers are achievable—and this book will give you the confidence and inspiration to realize your dreams.

Time marches on, and so do personal tastes. If you have purchased a new home, are preparing your home for life changes, need a room to function in a new way, or merely feel the urge to infuse your home with a new style, this book contains the inspiration and expert advice you need to make the change a reality. The focus of this book is redecorating, not time-consuming, costly remodeling that alters the structure of a room. You may be surprised how simple changes in surfaces—paint, fabrics, flooring, countertops—can take a room from woeful to wonderful.

To help you find the specific decorating ideas you want, this book of dramatic before-and-after transformations is organized by room. Within each section you will find a variety of home types, from old to new constructions, featuring different forms of architecture and decorated in all styles, including cottage, country, traditional, and contemporary. Even if you don't find a home or room that matches your own, the decorating principles at work will help you apply what you learn to your individual needs or project.

USE WHAT YOU HAVE

Sometimes the easiest way to make over a room is to use what you have in a new, innovative way. Many of the rooms pictured incorporate the existing furnishings and accessories, but fresh fabrics and paint bring new life to the space. Even simple changes in room arrangement that you can achieve in an afternoon can make your space more functional and appealing.

ONE ROOM TWO OR THREE WAYS

Options—that's what this book is about, so some rooms are shown redecorated in more than one way. This proves that good basic elements lend themselves to multiple decorating styles.

PROJECTS

You can certainly opt for store-bought decorating accessories, but why not make them yourself? This allows you to personalize ready-made items, often at a fraction of the price, and gives you a sense of pride for doing it yourself. Throughout this book, you will find dozens of projects, which range from pillow construction to beaded-board paneling installation. Many projects are presented with materials lists and step-by-step instructions that make completion quick and easy.

MORE IDEAS

Following each makeover you'll find additional information about one feature in that room—for example, lighting options for kitchens and bathrooms, or molding installations that add architectural interest in a living room. Look at the options and choose the one that best suits your home and lifestyle.

TRIED-AND-TRUE DECORATING TIPS AND TECHNIQUES

Want to know how to make a bedroom grow with your child or how to select the best paint color for a room? You will find the answers to your decorating questions in special sidebars throughout this book. These foolproof techniques and everlasting decorating principles will help you transform your home into the comfortable, stylish haven you've always dreamed of.

RESOURCES

Do you want the fabric or the paint color featured in one of the rooms? This section includes everything you need to know to find the materials you want quickly and easily.

Whether you want to turn your bedroom into a restful retreat or restyle your kitchen to make it a place where your family will want to linger long after a meal is over, this collection of inspiring makeovers will encourage you to get started today. The rooms are real, and the problems and solutions are believable. This is a book you will turn to again and again for practical advice and information to make your home a reflection of your personal style.

LIVING ROOMS

Arranged for the SEASONS

Updating a room for seasonal changes goes beyond decorative touches: Give your room a new attitude by moving the furniture to take advantage of all nature has to offer, bringing in colors and textures that reflect the time of year, and rethinking accessories. The best part? By using what you already have in innovative ways, you can capture the mood of the season.

In this long, narrow living room, a new furniture arrangement and a few seasonally appropriate touches create different looks for summer and winter. The furnishings and neutral-color slipcovers remain the same, resulting in an inexpensive afternoon makeover.

VERSION ONE: SIMPLY SUMMER

If you have a large picture window in your living room, make the most of the natural light and views it provides. In this room, two large sofas are positioned face-to-face in front of the window. This arrangement creates a conversation space for family and friends—and a comfortable place to catch a nap in the warm sun or read by natural daylight. A coffee table between the sofas provides a place to rest feet and set beverages.

Summery accessories set the tone. An additional conversation area camps in front of the fireplace. This intimate setting with two dark-color rattan chairs and a petite round table is ideal for casual dining. The shutters on the mantel evoke a feeling of breezy summer days. Other summery accessories include bright table linens, a vase of colorful flowers on the coffee table, and natural woven baskets that could easily be used for trips to the farmer's market.

Mix warm and cool colors. Colorwise, the white walls, warm wood floor (sans rug so that you can feel the cool, smooth floor under your bare feet), and neutral gray and eggplant-color slipcovers are a pleasing backdrop for crisp cotton pillows and vintage-look polka-dot-pattern throws in ocean blues, cream, and purple. This color scheme keeps the look cool and serene. Green, another "low-temperature" color, appears as an accent throughout the room. Orange and yellow, the complements of blue and purple, respectively, add a touch of warmth.

Continued on page 10

VERSION TWO: WINTER

VERSION ONE: SUMMER

VERSION TWO: WINTER WARMTH

When winter winds begin to howl and the temperature starts to drop, it's time to think about cuddling into comfort. Focusing on the fireplace, stashing summer fabrics and accents, and bringing in warm color accents and soft textures transform this room into an inviting haven from the cold.

Arrange the furnishings for function. The sofas stand back-to-back, creating distinct areas for different functions. The purple-covered sofa joins the two rattan chairs—now dressed with plump pillows—and coffee table for a cozy place to relax or converse around the warming glow of the fire. Graphic prints adorn the mantel: The bell pepper print sticks with the new color scheme and evokes memories of the season that recently passed. When the fireplace isn't in use, filling it with candles gives a pleasing glow. On the other side of the room, the gray-covered sofa faces a piano (not shown) in an intimate concert space.

Heat up the space with color. Warm color floods the space, from the red pillows to the orange-patterned rug beneath the gray sofa. Purple accents make an appearance in a pillow and throw, linking the two areas of the room and providing a splash of cool contrast. The tables are now uncovered, revealing warm wood tones.

Invite cozy comfort. Texture also defines this winter space. The summer arrangement featured crisp cottons and woven baskets; soft chenille pillows and throws pamper the space for winter.

NICE AND NEUTRAL

A neutral palette—dominated by white, cream, or brown—is very versatile, as this room demonstrates. These colors blend into the background, allowing the warm and cool colors to take center stage, and are able to temper dominant hues. To give a neutral scheme visual interest, introduce texture, such as wood furniture and woven baskets.

VERSION TWO: WINTER

VERSION ONE: SUMMER

WINTER WONDERLAND

Consider these strategies when planning a space for the winter months:

- **Color.** Neutrals work well as an overall palette. These colors can easily be accented with warm hues—red, orange, and yellow—to take the chill out of the room on cold winter days and nights.
- **Fabrics and Textures.** Bring out the flannel, wool, fleece, velvet, and chenille for snuggling.
- **Accents.** Light up a room with candles and sparkling ornaments in a bowl. Give a nod to Mother Nature with sprigs of holly and pine displayed on the mantel or in vases.

Seasonal Decorating

Spring. Summer. Autumn. Winter. When the seasons change, you have the opportunity to create an environment that reflects all of Mother Nature's splendor. At the onset of each season, look around and notice the colors, textures, and motifs that best reflect it. Think beyond traditional holiday decorating strategies. Assemble more universal collections that can be changed slightly for holidays, if desired. For example, the fall display *opposite above right* incorporates Halloween-motif items, such as a luminary, at the end of October and a cornucopia around Thanksgiving. The four examples shown here demonstrate how you can dress a mantel for each season. Follow these cues for tabletop and other displays throughout your home.

Spring. It's the time for new beginnings, so start on the right foot by filling a mantel with objects that invite light indoors. Eliminate dark, wintry decorations and bring in mirrors, empty glass containers that provide translucent sparkle, and fresh botanical prints.

Summer. Seaside symbols bring home the feeling of warm waves and ocean breezes—regardless of where you live. On this mantel, blond-wood frames resemble sun-bleached driftwood, and small buckets filled with sand and long grasses add breezy informality. Seashells complete the mood.

Autumn. When the leaves begin to change from green to brilliant oranges, reds, and yellows, look to Mother Nature for decorating inspiration. The focal point of this arrangement is a wreath placed off-center for an informal look. Copper vessels anchor the scene; melons, squashes, and pumpkins of varying sizes, colors, and textures fill in the spaces between. The slow-ripening produce can be used for seasonal recipes.

Winter. As the days grow short, find ways to take advantage of light. Glowing tea light candles line this mantel, and a taller candle hangs in front of the mirror. A winter landscape is further created by an oval-shape mirror, which looks like an icy pond. Topiary forms covered with miniature evergreen garlands and topped with red ribbons resemble tiny Christmas trees.

Stylish CHOICES

Sometimes one feature of a room is so overpowering it becomes difficult to see other possibilities. In this room the dominating feature was the dark green walls. The traditional-style accessories were compatible with the color, but they were too small—and there were too few to make an impact. Everything in the room seemed featherlight, too insubstantial to balance the weighty walls.

Identify key framework elements. Once the walls were "neutralized" with two coats of soft ecru-beige paint, style possibilities could be more easily determined. Three steps helped build the style foundation for the space. First, two parsons chairs and a large club chair (shown on page 18), which fit the scale for the room, are dressed in fresh, simple off-white slipcovers. The chairs are comfortably positioned to form two sides of a conversation grouping, creating a good layout for finishing the room. Second, the room's windows lacked coverings; sailcloth Roman shades installed inside the frames provide the background for tab-topped panels. Finally, the addition of a plain sisal rug completes the framework on the floor.

The two styles shown, contemporary and French, illustrate how to take those critical next steps to creating style in a neutral space.
Continued on page 16

BEFORE

VERSION ONE: FRENCH

VERSION TWO: CONTEMPORARY

VERSION ONE: FINELY FRENCH

This option gives the room a fresh approach to traditional. Pieces with curving lines and classic contours provide the French flavor. The warm cherry red from the toile curtains repeats in several pieces around the room to unify the space.

Accessorize with color, texture, and shape. One problem area is a long, blank wall. A white antique secretary and large oval mirror nicely fill the space while keeping the look light. Accent pieces in rattan add warm tones and gentle texture; iron pieces add curves and punctuating black touches. Cream-color curvy pitchers and urns are the perfect accessories to give this room a relaxed but stately feeling. For a little glimmer, silver vases and frames dot the room.

The sisal rug gets a celadon green banding to define the edges of the conversation grouping without adding too strong a color.

AFTER

BEFORE

Inside the antique secretary, contoured pottery, silver-tone frames, and old books complement the overall French feel of the room.

Cherry red and deep pink accents bring warm color into the mostly neutral space.

CREATING YOUR STYLE

Making big changes in a room that's firmly planted in one style can be a daunting task. Here are some ideas to help you formulate a new style for any room.

- **Go beyond neutral.** In this room, it would have been easy to stop with neutral everything—and after such an overwhelming wall color (dark green) such a decision would have been understandable. However, the room would have looked bland. If you start with a clear idea of the desired end result and work toward it, you'll have the motivation to complete the project.
- **Think of style as a layer.** If committing to upholstery, wall color, and window treatments in a particular style is more than you feel comfortable doing, create a neutral base, as was done here, and start choosing accessories and inexpensive, yet quality, furniture of a particular style for one area of the room. If you don't like it, your investment is minimal; if you do like it, you're halfway to completion.
- **Pick a point to start from—and follow it for every decision.** In this room, two approaches to defining a starting point are shown. In the contemporary version, a large painting is the key feature, setting the style and color selection. In the French version, the style itself guided the choices. Whatever your starting point, compare all your choices to it. You needn't follow a style or a color slavishly, but keeping your starting point as the focus helps unify the space.
- **Appreciate the good points.** Rarely is a room redecorated from scratch, and unless you do major remodeling, windows and doors will stay in place. So start on a positive note. This room had big windows and very nice seating pieces. Built from those elements, the makeover was easier to accomplish—and less expensive.
- **Pinpoint the trouble spots.** Note what makes a room uncomfortable and have a plan to deal with troublesome areas. Too much glare from the windows? Put filtering window treatments on the list. In this room, the wall color wasn't working, the windows needed subtle coverings, and a dark corner and long blank wall needed special attention. In the contemporary redo, the dark corner became a focal point; in the French-style redo, the long blank wall received two good-size pieces (the secretary and the mirror).

VERSION TWO: CONTEMPORARY CREATION

This style choice started with a dramatic abstract painting; the style of the room radiates from this focal point, formerly a dark corner. Peachy pink and light blue from the painting are repeated in fabrics and accessories throughout the room. The sleek torchiére indirectly lights the painting and illuminates the corner.

Bring purpose—and focus—to a corner. Four framed contemporary prints form a single visual unit on the long wall opposite the painting, and a trio of upholstered cubes take up residence underneath the drawings. These are multipurpose pieces: The cushioned tops pop off to reveal storage space, and the cubes can be pulled into seating service when needed. A large urn filled with curly willow branches adds height and texture to this corner—and balances the painting in the opposite corner.

Ground the design. Between the parsons chairs sits a glass-top table, an airy piece perfect in front of a window. It could, however, look too lightweight, so a light-color contemporary drawing is casually propped in the window to visually anchor the space.

Punctuate with black. In the center of the room, an ottoman draped with an animal-print throw sits on the sisal rug. The sharp angles of the decor are reflected in the black banding on the rug, and black accents spot the room to carry the contemporary theme.

Bring balance with simple window treatments. With strong style statements throughout the room, the curtains are subdued; simple sailcloth panels frame the windows.

BEFORE

AFTER

If luxurious fabrics such as silk are out of your price range, use them sparingly—as accents only—on pillows and other small items. This pillow has a quilted envelope fold and is embellished with a beaded tassel for a hint of romance.

FABRIC STRATEGIES

- The quality of upholstered furniture can vary. Pieces from the 1940s and 1950s often are constructed better than newer pieces; therefore, it might be worth spending the money to reupholster or slipcover them.
- Love an old sofa but not its droopy fabric and sagging seat cushions? If it has good lines and is well-constructed, a good workroom can add or replace batting and foam to make it comfortable again.
- Inexpensive fabrics can be enlivened with details. Chambray, twill, and cotton duck are sturdy, inexpensive materials that can be dressed up or dressed down. Trims, buttons, bows, and other dressmaker details can make plain fabric on a chair more interesting. Adding pillows covered in sumptuous fabrics is another way to dress up plain fabrics.
- If your windows are an odd size or have an odd configuration, don't assume that you'll have to have custom curtains made. Carry the measurements with you as you shop; you may be surprised by the variety of sizes of ready-made window treatments.

MORE IDEAS FOR

Freshening with Fabric

Fabrics, with all their pattern and color, have the power to transform a room. If your living room needs a punch of style, but you love your furnishings and the wall color, consider adding doses of fabric by way of slipcovers, pillows, window treatments, and small accessories such as lampshades and fabric-covered storage containers. When choosing fabric, consider the style of your room and how the room is used. For example, select tough, hard-wearing denim and corduroy if children frequently use the room. Antique fabrics with a faded, timeworn patina are perfect for window treatments and pillow covers in casual cottage-style settings.

If your living room suffers from textured drywall, cracked plaster, or dated paneling, hide the flaws with fabric. This stylish, drapey muslin panel swags between playful hooks screwed into a 1x4. This treatment provides the perfect camouflage for walls in need of repair. Coordinating checked fabric brings bold pattern to the window and chair cushion.

Loose, skirted chair slipcovers are an ideal choice for this relaxed cottage-style living room. The mix of patterned fabrics in similar colors—from florals of different sizes to the bold checks—adds interest to the room without overpowering it. The living room and adjoining kitchen are unified by the use of the same large floral-motif fabric on pillows and valances. See page 112 for more information on mixing fabric motifs and colors.

Fabrics can be more than slipcovers, window treatments, and other typical soft furnishings. If you have a prized collection of textiles, such as Native American blankets like those shown, antique quilts, or hand-dyed African fabrics, show them off! Hang them on rods or ladders propped against a wall. Frame those that are delicate or that require special care. Two caveats: To prevent fading, display textiles away from direct sunlight, and to avoid permanent creasing where textiles have been folded and hung, unfold them every so often and refold in a different way.

Fabrics in bright, sunny yellows and fresh pinks offset the dark wood-work and tiny windows in this living room. The slipcovers unite an assortment of traditional and contemporary furnishings. Patterned accent fabrics, such as covered lampshades and the banding on the sisal rug, add a feminine touch.

Boxy to BEAUTIFUL

You can revitalize any humdrum space—just take cues from this makeover. In this modular home, the living room is a boxy space with almost no architectural character. Adding visual interest is the key to making this a successful transformation; creating visual softness and defining a focal point are essential to the task.

Frame the space with wood. The thin walls in this home required attention first. They were originally covered with pale green painted paneling. Instead of ripping it down and starting from scratch, the paneling now wears a disguise of evenly spaced 1x4 boards, which make the old paneling seams less noticeable. The 60-inch-tall boards are capped with a plate rail, which runs around the perimeter of the room, providing visual interest and display space. The wall is topped with a hefty crown molding that visually flows right into the ceiling and is finished with an extra-tall baseboard. All the woodwork is painted a creamy white—a traditional cottage-style accent.

Create a sense of spaciousness. Although the ceiling is only 8 feet high in this room, the ornate moldings give it a grand appearance, and smart color choices make the space seem larger. Between the plate rail and crown molding, the walls are painted a deep purple; the ceiling is painted in a softer purple. This use of color visually heightens the walls and draws attention to the moldings.

Windows can take center stage. The wall with large windows had the potential of becoming a focal point, but there were no details to catch the eye. To start, new white energy-efficient windows are installed. For impact, boards are mounted between the windows, and a header is mounted above the windows to make them appear to be one unit. Simple wood blinds rather than window-blocking fabric treatments keep the focus on the architecture.

Continued on page 24

BEFORE

AFTER

Rethink furniture arrangement for increased function. After the "frame" of the room was complete, the furnishings and function of the space needed evaluation. Originally, the loves seat was floating in the room; it wasn't anchored to the chairs for a conversation grouping, and it was at an awkward angle for viewing the television. The newly slipcovered furniture pieces face the pine armoire, which moved from the corner to the wall adjacent to the windows. For additional

BEFORE

seating, a white bench (shown on page 23) joins the grouping. A large area rug, which is placed atop new neutral carpeting, anchors the arrangement.

Cottage-style colors and accents complete the look. The rug brings together the room's soft palette of cream, green, and purple. These three colors convene in a coordinated set of fabrics, which cover the love seat, chairs, and plump ottoman. The fabrics provide visual softness against the crisp, defined lines of the molding. The striped and floral fabrics are in scale with one another and set the stage for casual cottage-style accessories, including numerous shapes and sizes of candles, tin tiles that flank the armoire, and smooth-lined lamps and tables. Touches of silver join the mix in photo frames, lamp bases, and candle accessories.

Consider multifunction pieces. The finishing touch in this living room is the combination flip-top bench and coatrack, which provides practical storage. The bench serves as a convenient place to change footwear.

AFTER

Storage Box

This versatile storage box can work in any room of your home. It's a great place to stash stuff, and the top can serve as a place to sit to take off and put on shoes. This box has been mounted to the wall to appear as part of a single unit with the coat hooks above, but keeping it freestanding gives you the flexibility to move it where it's needed.

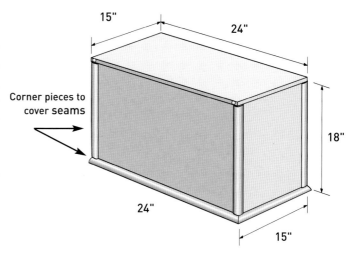

You Will Need

Poplar board cut to the following: 18x24" front and back (2); 15x18" sides (2); 15x24" top and bottom (2)
Hammer, nails
Trim, cut in sizes to cover corner seams
Wood glue
Sandpaper, primer, latex paint in the desired color and finish, paintbrush
2 piano hinges
Screwdriver, screws
2 glass beads, tacky glue

1 ▲ Construct the box by nailing together the front, back, sides, and bottom, following the illustration.

2 ▲ Apply trim to the box edges with wood glue, covering the seams.

3 ▲ Lightly sand the box and the top piece (lid). Prime; let dry. Paint; let dry.

4 ▲ Attach the lid to the box with the piano hinges. Mount the hinges on the inside of the box and underside of the lid.

5 ▲ To form the lip on the box lid, use tacky glue to attach a glass bead to each front corner on the underside of the lid.

15"   24"

Corner pieces to cover seams

18"

24"

15"

MORE IDEAS FOR

Adding Architecture with Moldings

Fresh from the lumberyard shelf, a combination of stock moldings in different shapes packs lots of personality for relatively little cost.

Built-in hutches are an asset to any home. Windowsill, Colonial, and standard molding pieces replicate a built-in hutch in this dining room; using the same wallpaper within the plate racks and below the chair rail enhances the illusion. For a similar look, draw the dimensions of the hutch on the wall; wallpaper within this area. Build the outer frame from poplar strips and cut windowsill stock for the shelves; paint the pieces and nail the shelves to the frame. Glue a piece of screen molding to the top of each windowsill piece, 2½ inches from the back, to form a lip. Mount the box to the wall. Cut the Colonial molding to fit the windowsill stock and paint each piece. Glue to the underside of each windowsill strip, aligning back edges. Attach quarter round to the front of the Colonial molding with glue and nails.

Vertical and horizontal molding strips can break up a tall wall, making it appear shorter. If you have high ceilings and want to visually shorten the walls, divide the wall horizontally; paint one color above the line and another below. For a look similar to this, paint dots in a contrasting color below the line. Cut screen molding strips to fit between the baseboard and where the under-cap molding will sit (at or near the line). Paint the screen molding, then glue and nail it to the wall, evenly spacing it. Cut the under-cap molding to fit the wall; paint, then glue and nail to the wall. Top the under-cap molding with painted doorstop molding cut to size.

Shaker pegs, topped with a shelf that's ideal for display space, act as hangers for photographs. To create this shelf, cut 1x8 pine boards the length of the wall; rip the boards to 4 inches wide for the shelf and 3⅜ inches for the peg rails. Paint the boards. Glue and nail the shelf to the rail, with the back edges flush at right angles. Cut decorative molding to fit the joint between the shelf and rail; paint, then glue and nail in place. Drill holes for the pegs, evenly spacing them along the rail. Mount the rail to the wall, drilling through some of the peg holes. Paint the pegs and glue in place.

Crisp and
CONTEMPORARY

Once a barren study space used as a pass-through, this room lacked real purpose. The challenge was transforming the under-utilized room into a functional space where people would want to linger. Help came in the form of paint, comfortable furnishings, and a mix of clean-lined contemporary accessories.

Mask damaged walls with paint. Romantic harlequin diamonds in a two-tone colorwash create a dramatic focal point in this room. Because the overall pattern is busy—and time-consuming to create—the treatment is reserved for one wall behind the sofa. The adjoining walls are painted in the darker of the diamond colors, keeping the focus on the pattern. The colorwashing technique is ideal for walls in ill condition, like the walls in this room: The paint will settle into any cracks and crevices, producing a highly textural appearance that enhances blemishes, making them a part of the design. The ceiling and crown molding have a fresh coat of white paint that visually lifts the ceiling.

Clean lines accentuate the focal point wall. The rich, warm color scheme on the walls defines the space and serves as a subtle backdrop for the brown upholstered sofa and chair and for natural wood furnishings in finishes from light to dark. The coffee table and metal-base lamps have a contemporary edge that blends well with the simple lines of the overstuffed sofa and chair. The clean lines throughout the room keep the attention on the diamond-painted wall. The area rug warms the wood floor and unifies the conversation grouping.

Continued on page 30

HOW COLOR AFFECTS A ROOM

When selecting paint colors for a room, first consider the size of your room, then decide whether you want to enhance its features or trick the eye into seeing the space in a different way. Follow these cues to help you select the colors that are right for your particular needs.

- **Closer** Warm colors advance, making walls seem closer.
- **Farther Away** Cool colors recede, making walls appear farther away.
- **Narrower** White or light-color ceilings make a room look narrower—and taller—when paired with dark walls.
- **Larger** Light-color walls make a room look larger because they reflect a lot of light rather than absorb it.
- **Lower** Dark painted ceilings visually make a room shorter.
- **Smaller** Walls in dark colors make a room appear smaller because they absorb light rather than reflect it.
- **Higher** White ceilings appear higher.
- **Wider** If you desire a wider-looking room, combine a dark ceiling with light walls.

BEFORE

AFTER

AFTER

Use shapes and lines as contrast. To keep the strong lines from making the room seem too hard-edged, plump pillows with stylized flowers grace the sofa. An oversize round clock, a graphic print on the desk (shown on page 29), and a tall floral arrangement with naturally flowing lines help balance the formal harlequin pattern.

The room still serves its original function (as an office), but now the space also is a place to relax or entertain.

▼

The defined lines of the painted harlequin diamond wall are balanced by accessories with soft curves, including the floral motif on the pillows.

 For more information on sensational paint treatments, visit **HGTV.com/beforeandafterbook**

Harlequin Diamond Walls

This classic design, with diamonds that are taller than they are wide, is versatile: Large or small, diamond patterns lend a sophisticated feel to rooms decorated in any manner. When choosing the size of your diamond pattern, keep the scale of the room and its furnishings in mind. Remember that the smaller the pattern, the more time-consuming the process will be (because you will need to measure, mark, and paint more diamonds). For ease in creating a diamond pattern, work with a partner and use a chalk line, as described below.

The diamonds in this living room/office are colorwashed in light and medium yellow for subtle contrast. For basic colorwashing, start with a light (white or cream) base coat and mix the top coat paint with glaze, a transparent medium that allows the paint to stay workable longer than plain paint. The glaze/paint mixture will create depth when applied to the walls with a sponge in circular strokes or with a paintbrush in a crosshatching motion. This design features two colors, but you can use a palette of colors for the technique.

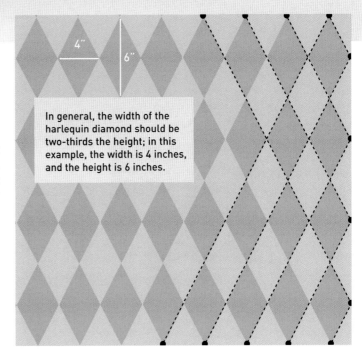

In general, the width of the harlequin diamond should be two-thirds the height; in this example, the width is 4 inches, and the height is 6 inches.

You Will Need

Satin or semi-gloss latex paint for
    base coat, white or cream
Satin or semi-gloss latex paint for
    top coat, two colors
Tape measure
Colored pencil that matches
    top coat paint
Chalk line
Optional: Painter's tape
Glaze
Bucket and mixing tool
Roller and paint tray
Paintbrushes or sea sponges

1 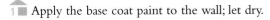 Apply the base coat paint to the wall; let dry.

2 Measure the height and width of the wall. Using these measurements, determine the size (height and width) of the individual diamonds in the design.

3 Using the illustration as a guide, measure and mark the width of the diamonds along the top and bottom of the wall using the tape measure and colored pencil. Measure and mark the height along each side in the same manner.

4 Working with a partner, snap a chalk line to join the marks. This creates the diagonal lines of the design.

5 If you desire crisp diamonds, use painter's tape to mask off (tape around as an outline to be filled in with paint) diamonds in the first color you would like to paint. If you

prefer a more freehand look, use the chalk lines as a guide. For either method, put a small piece of tape in the diamonds reserved for the second top coat color to prevent a pattern mishap.

6 Mix 4 parts glaze to 1 part top coat paint (first color).

7 Using either a paintbrush in a crosshatching X motion or a damp sea sponge in a circular motion, apply the glaze/paint mixture to the diamonds. Work quickly to ensure the mixture stays wet and workable. Remove painter's tape, if used, and let dry.

8 Remove the small pieces of tape in the remaining diamonds; mask off these diamonds if desired. Mix 4 parts glaze to 1 part of the second top coat paint. Paint the diamonds as in Step 7. Remove painter's tape, if used, and let dry.

MORE IDEAS FOR

Adding Drama with Paint

Any room will benefit from a fresh coat of paint, whether you're using a solid color or a decorative technique. Areas where people tend to gather, such as living and family rooms, are natural places to showcase color. Match colors and decorative techniques to the style of your room, taking cues from the furnishings, carpeting, window treatments, and accessories.

Embossed wallcoverings, available at specialty paint stores and home improvement centers, can be found in multiple motifs to suit nearly every decorating style. While the wallcoverings may be left white—or painted with a solid color of paint—using a squeegee to reveal the raised portions creates visual depth (the raised details stand out against the darker recessed areas). For this technique, first paint the wallcovering with a base coat of semi-gloss paint; let dry. Mix 1 part top coat paint (semi-gloss) with 4 parts glaze, paint over the base coat, and immediately remove some of the top coat glaze/paint mixture with a squeegee. In this contemporary living room, a light blue paint is used as the base coat; a darker blue top coat is used on portions of the wall, creating wide vertical stripes. A solid dark blue horizontal stripe breaks up the busy wall and serves as a stately backdrop for four framed photographs.

Polka dots make a lighthearted addition to a casual setting. In this room, inexpensive and easy-to-use dauber sponges, commonly used for stenciling and stamping, create layered dots. Paint the wall with the desired background color; let dry. Randomly paint dots onto the wall with one dauber; let dry. Using a marker, draw a row of scallops around the outer edge of another dauber and use scissors to cut along the line; draw and cut a row of scallops around the center, forming a ring. Use the cut dauber and another color of paint to stamp over the existing dots.

Fresco is a classic paint technique that can produce a contemporary feel, as in this spirited living area. Apply a layer of drywall joint compound to the wall, using a spackling knife and sweeping motions; let dry. Sand down protruding ridges and prime the wall with a high-nap roller. Paint the wall in a light base coat color like white or off-white; the top coat glaze/paint mixture will have more depth when applied over a light base coat. Mix a darker top coat color (1 part) with glaze (4 parts) and apply to the wall in a random fashion, allowing some of the base coat to show.

Easy-Going yet Elegant
FAMILY STYLE

BEFORE

Vaulted ceilings, big windows, and wood floors give the family room of this suburban home a lot of interest and plenty of light. The intent of this redo is to add that missing layer of comfort and ease that say "home." The challenge is creating the evolved look of casual style in a single pass.

Flowing window treatments balance distinct lines. A pretty, lightweight floral fabric serves as the window covering, which features several stylish design elements: The elegant draping swags capped with white decorative iron pieces celebrate the vaulted ceiling and the Palladian window's glorious height. The neatly pleated valances on all but the tallest window add a little structure. The combination of blinds and swags softens the sharp edges of the window frames and permits control of the bright sunlight that pours into the room. A warm taupe wall color accentuates the windows.

Consider all the elements in a room when hanging fixtures. A delicate Italian chandelier that's painted white brings the eye to the height of the Palladian window, but no higher. As one enters the room, the chandelier is perfectly framed by the window.

Classic cottage style: warm wood tones and pastels. Rich wood floors are easy to care for, a necessary asset for this busy room. They provide the perfect anchor for the white-slip-covered sofas and chair that make up the conversation area. The pink and white color scheme travels from the window treatments to throw pillows—plain and ruffled—in solids, prints, and checks. A whitewashed coffee table with a wood top centers the conversation group and firmly establishes the casual yet chic look.

Continued on page 36

AFTER

Curvy lines accentuate the space. Two corners of the room are softened considerably with a pair of round tables from the 1940s (shown on page 35). Painted creamy white, the tables feature curving legs and edges that perfectly complement this room and provide a stylish surface for delicate lamps embellished with crystal drops.

Give an armoire focal-point status. An antique armoire, also painted creamy white, stands against the one solid wall as a commanding but not overpowering focal point. The light color keeps the piece from looking top-heavy or bulky in this airy room. The recessed areas of the doors are covered in a delicately patterned wallpaper, adding elegant detail to the large armoire. Inside this older piece are the accoutrements necessary for the modern family room: video and stereo equipment. Storing these pieces behind doors keeps them readily accessible without allowing them to be the center of attention; that compromise maintains the beauty of the room without impeding the function.

Slipcovers can give importance. Although this room serves casual family needs, attention to detail fosters elegance. Consider, for example, the slipcover for the wing chair: Because this tall chair sits at the entrance to the room, the pleated skirt that wraps the bottom of the chair sits 4 inches off the floor. This gives the significant piece a lighter, airier look than if the slipcover draped to the floor, as those on the sofas do.

CREATING INFORMAL ELEGANCE

At first glance this room looks as though it has evolved easily into its casual, refined state. Even if the homeowners had had the leisure of developing the look over time, they would have employed many of the same principles (explained below) used in doing it all at once.

- **Choose core colors.** Choosing a white and pink theme accented with warm tones keeps the look clean, but choosing a basic color scheme in a room needn't tie you down. Rather, choose something that allows you creative flexibility while helping you focus on a final goal.
- **Fear not white!** Even though a rambunctious young family tramples through this room, white slipcovers work well. They are removable, so they can be washed easily when too many spills have occurred. The inviting drape of white slipcovers is casual, not sloppy, and the light color is an inviting backdrop for many styles.
- **Include dressmaker details.** Casually drooping slipcovers and loose swags of curtains are offset by the universal neatness accent: pleats. Pleated valances, slipcover skirts, and lampshades add visual order throughout the room.
- **Choose shapes that provide a framework for the space.** Keeping the sofas saved a lot of money, but on their own, the pieces are a bit nondescript. Accenting them with a wing chair, curvy end tables, and an armoire with graceful lines gives them—and the entire room—a more complete personality. The lamps and swagged curtains add complementary curving lines.

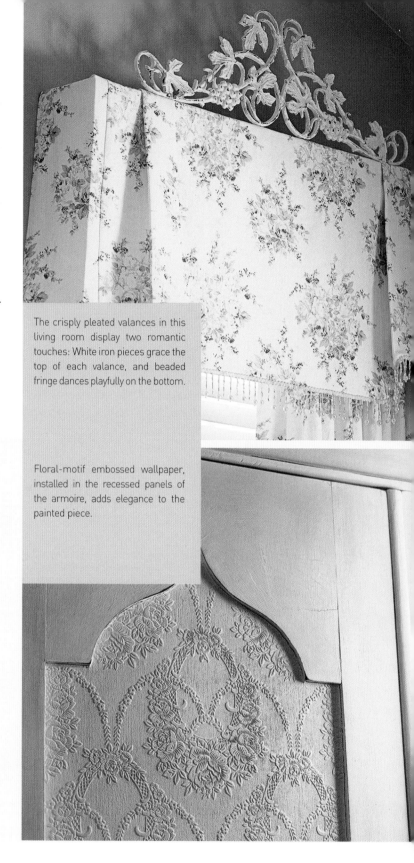

The crisply pleated valances in this living room display two romantic touches: White iron pieces grace the top of each valance, and beaded fringe dances playfully on the bottom.

Floral-motif embossed wallpaper, installed in the recessed panels of the armoire, adds elegance to the painted piece.

Painted and Papered Armoire

Wood armoires—vintage and new—make impressive focal points in any room. But when left unfinished, they can sometimes be more of an eyesore. Painting an armoire and adding a subtly patterned wallpaper to the recessed areas can make it a more pleasing focal point in your room.

You Will Need

Soap, water, bucket, rags
Wood putty, scraper
Fine-grit sandpaper, tack cloth
Paper, pencil, scissors
Embossed wallpaper, wallpaper paste, wallpaper smoother, sponge
Primer, latex paint in cream or white and any finish, paintbrushes
Brown glaze, rag

1 Remove the doors and drawers from the armoire. Thoroughly clean the armoire; dry.

2 Fill in any gouges, cracks, and holes with wood putty. When dry, sand to a smooth finish.

3 Sand the entire armoire to prepare it for painting. Using the tack cloth, remove any dust particles.

4 If your armoire has recessed panels similar to the ones pictured here, use paper and pencil to create a pattern for the wallpaper. Cut out the pattern and transfer it to the wallpaper; cut out.

5 Using wallpaper paste, adhere the wallpaper to the recessed panel. Carefully smooth out any wrinkles with a wallpaper smoother and use a damp sponge to wipe up any paste that has seeped from behind the paper. Repeat for all recessed areas.

6 Prime the armoire, including the recessed wallpapered portions; let dry.

7 Paint the armoire cream or white; let dry.

8 Sand the raised edges (i.e., corners) for a worn, distressed look.

9 Lightly rub brown glaze onto the armoire, including the wallpapered portions, to further age it.

MORE IDEAS FOR

Cottage-Style Decorating

Cottage style is all about calm, relaxation, and creating a retreat you can enjoy as an everyday getaway. Imagine your dream vacation home or ideal home-away-from-home: Is it a cottage on a lake you visited as a child? Or do you long for a rustic haven in the middle of the woods? Which elements do these places have? Comfortable furnishings that invite you to curl up in front of the fireplace with a good book? Vintage textiles, worn wood tables, and a soft color palette? Go to flea markets, thrift and antiques stores, and salvage yards to find charming timeworn furnishings and accessories that will transform your living spaces into the getaway you've always longed for.

Embellished pillows, furnishings painted a creamy white, and flea market finds fill this cozy, cottage-style living room. A mix of textures and architectural elements, from the gauzy fabric draped over the old three-panel floor screen to the large tin tile, gives the room a luxurious feel.

If your home lacks a porch, bring the outdoors in with wicker furnishings, vintage textiles, and garden-inspired accessories. Placing the chairs in front of the windows heightens the effect.

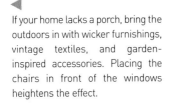

Cottage touches bloom on fabrics, hatboxes, and framed embroidery in this comfortable home. Distressed furnishings and found objects such as seashells complete the look. If you are unable to find authentic distressed pieces, see page 63 for instructions on giving wood furnishings and doors an aged, antique look.

It's all in the details: When decorating in a casual style, look for old discarded items such as this metal screen-door protector, which now serves as a place to display cherished photographs.

Designed for LIVING

Living rooms are used for many activities, including reading, relaxing, watching television, and a playspace for children. It's little wonder, then, that these rooms often become cluttered with books and magazines, audiovisual equipment, and toys. Finding stylish storage solutions can be a problem, but this living room handles it with grace. A bookcase is converted into an entertainment center that conceals the television when it's not in use; footlockers covered in imitation suede become deep storage chests that also serve as extra seating; new benches that flank the fireplace corral CDs and magazines.

Punch up the scheme with a mix of color and pattern. Storage wasn't the only challenge, however. The nearly monochromatic scheme lacked excitement—green covered the walls, furnishings, and accessories, accented only by cream. The fresh, light green is still the foundation for the scheme in the newly transformed space, but lavender accents and a mix of striped, floral, and solid fabrics enliven the room. A custom floorcloth replaces the chenille rug and anchors the room by bringing together all the colors in the furnishings, fabrics, and accessories.

Ample seating for all. Because this room hosts many visitors, sufficient seating space is a must. The green chair is still in place, but the old taupe sofa has been replaced with a larger, more comfortable cream-color sofa. The benches placed on each side of the fireplace and the ottomans set on casters provide seating and practical storage; both can be moved around the room to suit various needs and configurations. Piles of pillows beckon guests to the seating pieces; they also can be tossed on the floor for casual seating.

Draw attention to the fireplace. Originally, the fireplace, the focal point of the room, stood out against the unadorned green walls, but it lacked emphasis because of mismatched, cluttered accessories set atop the mantel. The mantel display is now simplified with three clean-line vintage vases; on the wall four photographs transferred onto canvas flank the mantel. A stack of hatboxes covered in art papers provides additional storage and can even serve as an impromptu end table.

PAINTED FLOORCLOTHS

Floorcloths are an inexpensive, easy way to add style, color, and pattern to any room. Preprimed canvas—canvas treated with artist's gesso—is available by the yard, by the ounce, per square foot, or by a number and name at crafts and art supply stores (the higher the number, the stronger the canvas). Cut canvas to the desired size and shape with scissors or a rotary cutter, or purchase precut canvas, such as rectangles and circles. Most canvas is nonfraying, but some types may require "hemming" with an adhesive, such as hot glue. This floorcloth is divided into 11½-inch squares and painted with acrylic paint in dark and light lavender, green, teal, and cream (note that latex paint also may be used); the crisp lines are created with the aid of painter's tape. To protect a floorcloth against wear, two coats of clear acrylic polyurethane are applied to the top.

 For additional floorcloth ideas and projects, visit **HGTV.com/beforeandafterbook**

BEFORE

AFTER

Storage Bench

Stylish storage is easy to create: With bullnose wood panels and a couple of hours you can build a simple bench that can be used for storage and seating.

You Will Need

3/4" bullnose wood panels, cut to the following: 33x11¼" seat and bottom shelf (2); 21x11¼" sides (2)
Pencil
Drill or screwdriver
2" wood screws
Optional: L brackets

Wood putty, scraper
Sandpaper, tack cloth
Primer, latex paint in the desired color and finish, paintbrush
11¼x33x3" piece of foam
1 yard decorator fabric, 45" wide
Scissors, needle, matching thread

1 ■ Following the illustration, make pencil lines on the side panels where the seat and bottom shelf will be.

2 ■ Drill pilot holes on each side panel, where they will be attached to the shelves.

3 ■ Screw the shelves to the side panels. If additional support is needed, attach L brackets.

4 ■ Using wood putty, fill in the gaps where the shelf meets each side panel at the front bullnose; let dry.

5 ■ Lightly sand the bench; remove dust with the tack cloth. Prime; let dry. Paint; let dry.

6 ■ Wrap the fabric around the foam as if wrapping a present; trim excess fabric. Secure the fabric to the underside of the foam with a few stitches. Place the covered cushion on the bench seat.

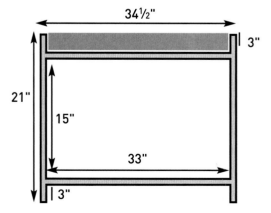

Trunk Ottoman

Ottomans can be more than a place to rest your feet; they can provide hidden storage. For an affordable storage ottoman, take a footlocker or trunk and cover it in soft, strong, nonfraying imitation suede.

You Will Need

Trunk or footlocker (the top of this
    example is 16x30")
Pencil or marker
Latex paint to match faux
    suede, paintbrush
2" thick foam, cut to fit top of
    footlocker or trunk
Quilt batting to cover sides and
    top of trunk
Staple gun, staples
Screwdriver or drill
4 screw-in casters with screws/nuts
2 yards faux suede in the desired color
Scissors
Long needle, matching thread
Thin-gauge wire
Straight pins
1 drawer pull
Braided trim to match faux suede
10 buttons with shanks to match
    faux suede

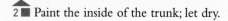

1 ■ Mark the location of the hinges on the inside of the trunk. Remove all hardware (handles, hinges and latches) from the trunk or footlocker.

2 ■ Paint the inside of the trunk; let dry.

3 ■ Place the foam on top of the lid. Center six layers of quilt batting on top of the foam. Cut a small square from each corner of batting so that it easily folds around the foam and lid; staple batting to the sides of the lid, keeping in mind that too many staples can create a rippled effect when the faux suede is pulled taut inside the lid.

4 ■ Staple four layers of batting to the outside of the trunk.

5 ■ Turn over the trunk. Predrill holes for the casters; screw the casters into place.

6 ■ Cut the faux suede to cover the top and sides of the trunk. Place the fabric right side down on top of the trunk. Pin the corners to sew a seam and create a fitted top; turn right side out and slip over the top of the trunk. Staple the fabric to the inside of the trunk lid, pulling the fabric taut.

7 ■ Cut slits for the hinges on the back of the trunk; fold any excess fabric up and under.

8 ■ On the inside of the trunk lid, drill 10 holes for tufting (every 5 inches in two rows). Using a long needle and long double thread, place the needle into the hole and bring through the lid. Place thin-gauge wire into the needle hole and pull the needle back through hole with thread. Take out the wire, thread the button, and poke the shank through to the top. Place the button on the thread, pull the thread tight to tuft, and tie off, clipping the threads close to the button. Repeat for each button.

9 ■ For the sides, sew the front and one side piece of the faux suede together with right sides facing. Repeat with the back and remaining side piece. Place the fabric on the trunk; pin the pieces together to create a fitted slipcover; remove. Sew the two sections together, place on the trunk, and staple to the inside. Check that the fabric is even around the bottom as you staple to the inside of the trunk.

10 ■ Attach the drawer pull to the center front of the trunk lid.

11 ■ Cut the braided trim into pieces to cover the inside of the trunk and lid. Glue the pieces in place over the staples.

12 ■ Reattach the trunk hinges in the marked locations (Step 1).

MORE IDEAS FOR

TV Storage

Convenience and easy viewing are priorities for rooms that house televisions and audiovisual equipment, but when these items are located in the main living area, they tend to take center stage. If you love watching movies and catching up on the latest news, and you aren't willing to find another location for the TV, at least make its presence more discreet. If you have an entertainment center, consider adding doors or a fabric curtain to hide the equipment when it's not in use. Scout out underused space—for instance, beneath a staircase—to keep the room's attention on furnishings, artwork, and collections.

A niche for a television and stereo equipment makes the most of space beneath the stairs in this home. Doors hide the equipment when it's not in use. When planning spaces for electronic gear, allow for the manufacturer's suggested ventilation space and for electrical outlets and appropriate wiring.

Although this fireplace is no longer used for its original purpose, it still has an important function: The doors above the circa-1850 mantel conceal a television.

Armoires are wonderful places to store televisions and related equipment: Doors hide what's stashed within, and myriad techniques can be used to make even the most ordinary armoire a striking focal point in any room. The nature-inspired color scheme and motif painted on this armoire blend in with the knotty pine paneling and lodge-look accessories. See page 37 for an armoire that has been whitewashed and wallpapered to suit a cottage-style setting.

KITCHENS &

DINING ROOMS

Light but not WHITE

D esign axioms are best interpreted rather than blindly applied. For example, "use white to make a space look larger" can sometimes create a stark and boring room if you follow only the letter of the law. Instead, select an eye-pleasing blend of light tones. In this tiny condo kitchen, a $1,000 makeover created a space that's bright, inviting, and functional.

Warm the space with color and wood tones; add visual punch with hardware. A "butter and cream" combination of mellow white and soft yellow paint softens the harsh contrast of heavily grained oak cabinets and muddy-blue walls. The repositioned refrigerator and ominously black dishwasher receive coverings to reduce their visual prominence. Large, shiny drawer and cabinet pulls make way for small, brushed-silver-tone knobs that do the job inconspicuously. New wood laminate flooring topped with an apple green rug completes the surface warming.

Good lighting is a kitchen essential. With two doors but no windows, the room required a good lighting plan. The soft yellow walls and one-shade-from-white cabinets stretch and soften the light from existing sources: a ceiling fixture, a fluorescent strip over the sink, and a single-bulb fixture in the stove hood. To improve the countertop lighting, two brushed-nickel lamps stand at the ready, an unexpected but elegant addition to the lighting pool.

Keep an eye on the details. Because everything is exposed in a small kitchen, think aesthetics as well as function. The new faucet upgrades the plain stainless-steel sink. New towels and a rug complement the new look. The lamps and a gathering of simple white pitchers pretty up the countertop landscape. A wood stool provides a handy place to sit but easily can be moved out of the way when the cooking action heats up.

BEFORE

AFTER

Lamps with brushed-nickel bases and understated white shades add elegant task lighting. The lamp base complements other brushed-nickel elements in the room, including the new faucet (shown below).

The top of this refrigerator is used as storage space; keeping the items in baskets reduces clutter.

SIZEWISE

- In a small kitchen, appliances can visually dominate and make the room feel crowded. Here, turning the refrigerator 90 degrees increases the usable floorspace and downplays the visual impact of the appliance. Covering the black facade of the dishwasher with a custom panel makes it blend neatly with the freshly painted cabinetry.
- Baskets maximize the storage potential of the refrigerator. A large wicker basket tucked in the back corner stores paper towels, a second basket holds other kitchen essentials, and a small basket-tray at the fore holds bottled water. When the design or packaging of a product looks good, use it as part of your display (especially in a grouping like the water bottles on top of this refrigerator) to free up precious closed-cabinet storage space.
- If your space is small, you may be able to splurge on one item, such as flooring or countertops, because you don't need much of it. About half the budget in this makeover went for flooring labor and materials.

Refrigerator Bulletin Board

If one side or both sides of your refrigerator is exposed, this is a great project to put that unused space to good decorative use.

You Will Need

36x48" bulletin board
Newspapers or other
  protective floor covering
Matte spray paint, black or
  other desired color
Tape measure
Scissors

1½ yards fabric, in the desired
  color and motif
Spray adhesive
Tacky glue
Decorative buttons
Brass thumbtacks
Double-sided carpet tape

1 Place the bulletin board on the newspapers or other protective floor covering.

2 Carefully paint the frame of the bulletin board; let dry and spray a second coat. **Note:** *It doesn't matter if paint gets on the bulletin board portion, because it will be covered with fabric.*

3 Measure the bulletin board portion (inside the frame). Get the exact measurement so the fabric will completely cover the area. Cut the fabric to this size.

4 Thoroughly spray the bulletin board portion with spray adhesive, following the manufacturer's instructions. Starting at the top left corner, carefully press on the fabric, smoothing it so there are no bubbles.

5 Using tacky glue, adhere the decorative buttons to the brass thumbtacks. Press the buttons along the outer edge of the bulletin board to resemble upholstery tacks.

6 Turn the bulletin board over. Attach double-sided carpet tape around the outside edges. Adhere the bulletin board to the side of the refrigerator.

Dishwasher Panel

Creating a panel to disguise an off-color dishwasher is an inexpensive alternative to having a panel custom-made or purchasing a new dishwasher. This example has been painted to resemble the cabinets, but you could top the panel with magnetic or chalkboard paint to make a child's drawing space. If you do not own a saw to cut the plywood and lathing strips, note that many home improvement centers will make cuts free of charge or for a minimal fee; mitered cuts may cost extra.

You Will Need

Tape measure
½" plywood
Optional: Saw, miter saw
1" lathing strips
Wood glue
Finishing nails

Hammer
1½" molding that matches cabinetry
Sandpaper, tack cloth
Primer, latex paint in the desired
  color and finish, paintbrush
Hook-and-loop tape
Scissors

1 Measure the exact length and width of the dishwasher front. Cut the plywood to these measurements.

2 Measure the length and depth of the dishwasher sides, top, and bottom. **Note:** *This measurement is usually about 1 inch deep by the same length (sides) or width (top and bottom) as the dishwasher front.* Cut lathing strips to match each measurement.

3 Glue the lathing strips to each side of plywood front piece. Secure in place with several finishing nails on each side.

4 Using the measurements from Step 1, miter four pieces of molding to fit the plywood panel. Glue the mitered pieces to the panel; let dry.

5 Sand the panel; remove dust particles with the tack cloth. Prime; let dry. Paint; let dry.

6 Attach hook-and-loop tape to the back of the panel and to the front of the dishwasher so that the tape aligns. Press the panel to the dishwasher front.

MORE IDEAS FOR

Lighting

Lighting is a major consideration for any kitchen. Kitchens require a blend of general, task, and accent lighting, with each type serving a different need. General or ambient lights provide a uniform, overall glow. Task lights are positioned to give light where you need it for specific jobs, for instance, doing dishes or chopping vegetables. Accent lights focus light on an object or surface to highlight it.

Unobtrusive recessed can lights are a popular choice for all three types of lighting. Can lights are available in downlight, accent, and wall-washing models. Track lights are another versatile option: Because the lights swivel on the track, they can be used for general, task, and accent needs. Pendent lights are another popular choice. Hung from a ceiling, pendants can be used for general and task lighting; when grouped, they are a great choice above islands and tables. Finally, undercabinet fixtures provide wonderful task lighting. These fixtures include slim energy-efficient fluorescents, miniature track lights, and strips of low-voltage mini halogens.

An average-size kitchen, measuring about 120 square feet, requires approximately 150 to 200 watts of incandescent general lighting, or 60 to 80 watts of fluorescent lighting. For larger kitchens, allow 2 to 3 watts of incandescent light or $\frac{3}{4}$ to 1 watt of fluorescent light per square foot.

Three pendent fixtures over the island provide light where it's needed most. Recessed can lights provide general lighting, while undercabinet fixtures create additional task lighting.

Accent lighting is a great way to bring focus to prized collections. Items on display in a niche get special attention, thanks to a single accent light.

Lights tucked inside glass-fronted cabinets offer a warm glow; glass shelves allow the light to flow through the cabinet. Note the recessed task lighting above the countertop run.

Sunshine can provide lovely ambient light in kitchens with large windows.

LIGHTBULBS

Choosing the correct bulbs will make your general, task, and accent lighting as efficient and effective as possible. Keep the following in mind the next time you shop for lightbulbs.

Incandescent These bulbs traditionally are used throughout the home. While they are inexpensive, they produce more heat than light, so they are inefficient unless used only sparingly.

EnergyMiser or Supersaver This type of incandescent bulb uses 5 to 13 percent less energy than a traditional incandescent. These bulbs cost a little more than the traditional type, but their longer life makes them more cost-effective.

Halogen These bulbs are more efficient than incandescents: They last three to four times longer, and a lower-wattage halogen bulb will give the same illumination as a larger-watt incandescent.

Compact fluorescent These bulbs screw into the same sockets as incandescents but use about 75 percent less energy than incandescent bulbs—and last 10 times longer. They can be expensive, but over time they save many times their initial cost.

Linear fluorescents These thin tubes produce even, glare-free, shadow-free illumination, which is ideal for general lighting. Linear fluorescents also can be used for undercabinet lighting.

A large pendant light provides general lighting in this contemporary kitchen. A light-color ceiling and pale flooring prevent the black cabinets and countertops from absorbing too much of the light.

Sleek Design on a BUDGET

Even the most budget-conscious kitchen remodeling projects require thoughtfulness and care. In this kitchen, the main objective was refreshing the surfaces (walls, floors, and countertops), but three smaller details—covering an unsightly electrical box, consolidating cooking appliances, and creating a clever window treatment—completed the transformation.

Initially, the soffit and cabinets were painted white, a blue and white border circled the room, and a gray laminate covered the entire backsplash. The white laminate counters were showing their age, as was the vinyl flooring that had a sad coat of paint over it.

PAINTING CABINETS

A fresh coat or two of paint is a cost-effective way to dress up a dreary kitchen. A little prep work will make the job last.

- Determine which type of paint is on the cabinets: Put rubbing alcohol on a clean rag and wipe an inside surface. If the paint comes up, it's latex (water-base); if the paint is unaffected, it's alkyd (oil-base). You can paint oil over latex, but only certain latex paints will adhere to oils, so check the label before you buy.
- Some paints are designed to stand up to the moisture and temperature changes in kitchens and baths. These usually cost a little more but are worth the expense. A smooth paint finish will make kitchen cleanup easier; eggshell and semi-gloss paints fit the bill, without giving the excess shine of gloss paint.
- Thoroughly clean cabinets to remove dirt and cooking grease residue. Trisodium phosphate (TSP) is a popular cleaning agent.
- If you're replacing cabinet hardware, patch the old holes.
- Lightly sand the surface and prime to help the new paint adhere.

Pull the look together with paint and wallcoverings. To give the room a unified appearance, the cabinets and soffit were painted a soft, neutral beige. A commercial-grade vinyl wallpaper embellished with silvery squares covers the backsplash. The overall environment of the kitchen is addressed in applying these elements: A wallpaper paste designed for humid conditions was used to attach the wallpaper. The counter edge of the wallpaper is protected with a strip of quarter round that's held firmly in place with waterproof caulk.
Continued on page 56

BEFORE

AFTER

The new flooring is actually vinyl tiles that have the look of authentic terra-cotta tiles—and cost just a fraction of the real thing.

Easy-care commercial-grade wallpaper that is decorated with a silvery square motif covers the backsplash. The wallpaper echoes the kitchen's new brushed-metal accents.

Versatile vinyl. The old flooring was scraped down to the concrete subfloor. New high-quality vinyl tiles with the look of terra-cotta now cover the floor and give the room a warm glow. In an older house, vinyl tile is a good choice: After you've made the subfloor as clean and level as possible, remaining imperfections will be hidden by the flexible vinyl (ceramic tiles may break). Vinyl tile also is easy to install.

Cost-effective countertop. Because the existing countertops were structurally sound, new granite-look laminate has been glued directly over the surface. To ensure a smooth, seamless look, a professional tackled the job; the gleaming results reflect the skill of the artisan.

Copper fusion. The warm tone of the flooring repeats throughout the kitchen. The counter laminate has flecks of coppery terra-cotta. New copper-tone cabinet pulls decorate drawers and doors. The window treatment deserves kudos for cleverness: A sheet of copper screen wire was folded and crinkled to look like a sheet curtain. This shimmery curtain welcomes the breeze and lightly filters sunlight.

Conceal an eyesore. A custom cover disguises the unsightly electrical box. Because the box was in so obvious a location (next to the sink), wallpaper with a swirl pattern in copper tones was applied on the front panel; a strip of hooks was added below to make the space useful.

Consolidation equals efficiency. New surfaces can give a kitchen a unified look, but they don't change the functionality of the space. This kitchen already worked quite well. Cabinets provided sufficient storage and the major appliances were positioned effectively. However, one simple change perfected the setup: The varying cabinet heights create a few odd voids along the walls, and one of those open spots was right next to the wall oven. That's where a shelf was added for the microwave; the bread machine found a new home in the same corner; thus, a neatly consolidated cooking area was created.

Crinkly Copper Wire Curtain

If you are looking for a nonstandard, nonfabric window treatment, consider this clever option.

You Will Need

Tape measure
Optional: work gloves
Aluminum or copper screen wire
Utility scissors or knife

Optional: Spray paint, copper or other desired color
Cafe curtain brackets
Screwdriver
Dowel rod cut to the desired width

1. Measure the window length and width. Unroll the screen wire and cut to match the height of the window plus ½ inch; then cut across so the screen is double the width of the window plus 1 inch. Fold the cut edges ½ inch. **Note:** *The factory edge can be used as a finished edge.*

2. If desired, spray-paint both sides of the screen; let dry.

3. Crumple the screen to give it a wrinkled look. Gently flatten and accordion-fold the screen. **Note:** *If you've painted the screen, a little paint may flake off.*

4. Attach the brackets to the wall or window frame.

5. Cut an X at the top of each fold in the screen. Run the dowel rod through the holes and hang the rod in the brackets.

3

✳ For additional window treatment projects, including shades, curtains, and valances, visit **HGTV.com/beforeandafterbook**

MORE IDEAS FOR

Backsplashes

Backsplashes play an important role in the kitchen: They stop messy spills, splashes, and splatters from seeping behind the cabinets. It's a messy job, but that doesn't mean backsplashes can't be beautiful. Backsplashes come in many styles and materials, from popular ceramic tile and treated beaded board to more exotic glass and granite, so they can be as attractive as they are functional.

Ceramic tiles of all shapes, sizes, and motifs can be used effectively as a backsplash. The large tiles shown here were inspired by 1920s seed packets. Search tile stores and home improvement centers for the right tiles for your decorating scheme.

Wood usually isn't associated with areas that receive frequent washings, but if you treat it with a coat of polyurethane, it will perform beautifully. Beaded-board backsplashes look particularly at home in country decorating styles.

Granite often is used for countertops because of its durability. However, it rarely is seen as a backsplash. Here, a type of granite known as emerald pearl covers both surfaces (see page 71 for a larger look at this kitchen). Pieces of mica create the sparkle in the dark material.

This painted masterpiece was created on artist's canvas and adhered to the wall with wallpaper paste. Three coats of polyurethane protect the acrylic paint from the elements, and a narrow row of glazed tiles with a leaf motif anchors the canvas to the counter.

Copper in any form brings warmth to a kitchen. The patina on this golden copper backsplash provides a rich backdrop for cherry cabinets.

Mosaics are an artistic take on the backsplash. This example is made from broken tiles and found objects such as seashells. The dark grout helps to hide food splatters, and the shelf above displays dishware.

Mix-It-Up MAKEOVER

Sometimes a room is so dark, dull, and outdated it's hard to know where to begin, especially when the budget is tight. If you are faced with a similar situation, take heart: By evaluating what works—and what doesn't—and thinking about ways to freshen items that still function but aren't aesthetically pleasing, you can transform a space for a lot less money than you might think.

Update with paint. In this kitchen the cabinets had to be addressed first. Purchasing new cabinets is costly: They can consume up to 40 percent of a kitchen remodeling budget. Why not dedicate that money to other uses—such as new appliances—or even keep the money in your pocket by painting your existing cabinets and replacing the hardware? That's what was done here: Two colors—sunny yellow and barn red—now cover the cabinets in a distressed finish. The red paint could have been overpowering, but it is covered with a dark stain, which softens the look. New, clean-lined hardware in brushed nickel adds a sleek, contemporary edge, which contrasts nicely with the paint treatment.

Smooth transitions. The fresh-looking vinyl floor was retained, but the dark backsplash tiles and worn laminate countertops needed to be replaced. The tiles were removed, and the backsplash area now wears a traditional red and white toile-print wallpaper. The print adds visual interest to the space and complements the red and yellow painted cabinets. A single row of white ceramic tile functions as a short, easy-clean backsplash. To reduce project costs, the existing counter stays put, but it's now covered with a light wood-tone laminate. The edge is painted red and distressed for a seamless transition between the counter and the cabinets below.

Continued on page 62

CABINET HARDWARE

One of the easiest ways to add a spark to cabinets is with hardware. The selection available at home improvement centers and through Internet or mail-order sources is impressive. Styles include metal shapes with interesting curves and ceramic knobs and pulls with painted-on motifs. Wood knobs can be personalized with paint that complements the cabinets and overall decorating style.

BEFORE

AFTER

Dress the window for success. The once bare window over the sink now is dressed with a matchstick wood shade. The textured treatment is a fun, natural touch that adds contemporary flair to the overall traditional scheme. The white-painted window frame blends with the newly decorated space.

Appliances blend in for a seamless look. Because the homeowners saved money by salvaging the cabinets (the doors had been removed and were retained for reuse) and flooring and covering the countertop, they purchased new white appliances—a dishwasher, range, and microwave oven—that give the room a more uniform look; the dark dishwasher and range would have drawn too much attention in the now lighter, brighter space.

Pay attention to details. As in many rooms, it's the finishing touches that pull a look together, and this kitchen is no exception. A brushed-nickel gooseneck faucet, red and white collectibles and ceramic pieces, and a white chair that's handy for sorting mail or looking for a recipe unify the space.

BEFORE

AFTER

PROJECT

Distressed Cabinets

Refreshing tired cabinets or giving brand-new cabinets an aged appearance is easy. When selecting colors, remember that the base coat color will only peek through the top coat where the top coat is sanded away. For an authentic aged appearance, do most of the sanding where natural wear would occur—for instance around handles and on raised portions of the project surface.

You Will Need

Screwdriver
Latex primer
Medium-grit sandpaper, tack cloth
Paintbrushes, paint tray
Latex paint for base coat in the
  desired color and finish

Latex paint for top coat in the
  desired color and finish
Water-base stain in desired finish
Lint-free cloths
Wax or water-base polyurethane

1. Remove the doors and drawers from the cabinets. Remove any hardware.

2. Prime the cabinets, doors, and drawer fronts; let dry.

3. Lightly sand the surfaces. Wipe away dust with a tack cloth.

4. Apply the base coat to all surfaces; let dry.

5. If desired, apply wax to the surfaces.

6. Apply the top coat paint to all surfaces; let dry.

7. Sand the raised portions of the door and drawer surfaces as well as the cabinet edges, rubbing away paint in the natural wear areas. Wipe away dust with a tack cloth.

8. Randomly brush stain onto one area of one surface. Quickly wipe away some of the stain with a lint-free cloth, allowing the stain to sink into the recessed areas. Continue applying and removing stain until the entire surface has been covered. Repeat for the doors, drawers, and cabinet surfaces.

9. Rub the painted surface with wax or apply polyurethane for protection.

7

8

MORE IDEAS FOR
Cabinet Doors

Cabinets can consume a large part of any kitchen makeover budget, so if your existing cabinets still function well, consider some easy updates: Paint them. Remove the doors and add fabric curtains. Incorporate inserts of nearly any material on the doors. Add new pulls and knobs.

Decades ago, glass inserted into a cabinet door was most prized for its practicality: You could see what was inside the cabinet without opening the door. Glass is now also valued for the many looks it can create. In this kitchen, complete with stainless-steel appliances and soapstone countertops, frosted glass enhances the contemporary feel. Other options include various glass colors and patterns and art paper laminated between glass layers.

Old, dingy cabinets get a fresh coat of paint and well-placed fabric details in this 1917 kitchen. The blue and white color scheme was inspired by a border of delft accent tiles. Coordinating delft fabric dresses the windows and lines the glass-fronted upper cabinets. Strategically placed fabric covers unsightly areas: A pretty pleated skirt hides lower cabinets made of metal.

Placing inserts in cabinet doors is a great way to add charm—and to replace worn surfaces. Most commonly, inserts are made of beaded board, glass, or even wallpaper that covers a portion of the door. Punched and painted tin is a less common material that adds flair to any kitchen. The tin inserts here feature Mexican motifs, a perfect complement for the backsplash tiles.

Style on the
SURFACE

Kitchens—along with bathrooms—are the most often remodeled rooms of the home, but updating them doesn't have to entail costly demolition. As this kitchen demonstrates, rethinking surface treatments, including wallcoverings, cabinet doors, hardware, and countertops, can refresh a tired space within the existing floor plan. This saves time, money, and the inconveniences that accompany more extensive remodeling.

Fresh color and interesting motifs set the stage. First, a light-color striped wallpaper replaces fruit motif paper. The light walls keep the small room from seeming even smaller, and the vertical stripes visually lift the ceiling, which is now covered in a dramatic chocolate brown wallpaper with an intricate swirling design. This design repeats in decorative elements throughout the room, including the rustic-looking chandelier that provides much-needed light above the island.

Continued on page 68

KITCHEN COMFORT

Living rooms are the obvious conversational center of a home, but kitchens are a natural gathering place. In fact, a recent study shows that during waking hours, people tend to spend more time in the kitchen than any other room of the home. What can you do to encourage family and friends to linger while you cook and after a meal is served?

- **Pull up a chair.** If you have an island or a peninsula, arrange stools or high-back chairs around it to allow people to socialize while you cook. Guests can be close to the cook without interfering with meal preparation or traffic flow.
- **Personalize it.** Kitchens often open or flow into other living spaces, so decorate accordingly. Paint. Add pattern. Incorporate fabric. Showcase a collection. When your kitchen is filled with what you love, it becomes a welcoming place—a home within a home for you and your family and friends.
- **Set the mood.** Put on some music that suits the occasion. Get your family or guests involved in making the meal. They can set the table or chop vegetables while you prepare the main dishes. Keep snacks and beverages close at hand. Provide adequate lighting for special activities, for instance, overhead lighting above a table if you want to play after-dinner board or card games.

BEFORE

AFTER

Casual country style. Newly installed beaded board dramatically changes the overall look of this now fresh country kitchen. Cut to fit between the cabinets and countertops, ¼-inch beaded-board panel is glued on top of the existing laminate back-splash; the rest is cut to size and glued into the recessed areas of the cabinet doors. The birch cabinets were previously left with a natural finish; now they sport an aged glazed finish. Two coats of polyurethane protect both the backsplash and cabinets from splatters.

Creative countertop. The once plain laminate countertop now has a custom look, thanks to 15-inch glazed tiles in a rustic blue that complements the aged cabinets. The tiles were first set on the countertop to determine a pleasing arrangement; then the corner tiles were cut to size and the tiles were attached to the countertop with thin set. A light sand-color grout fills in the spaces between the tiles. To complete the look, flexible trim painted to match the aged cabinets covers the laminate edge.

Pull the look together. For added style, the porcelain cabinetry knobs have been replaced with stylish wrought iron, which complements the new iron light fixture over the island. The island chairs are spiffed up with distressed blue paint finish similar to the color of the glazed countertop tiles.

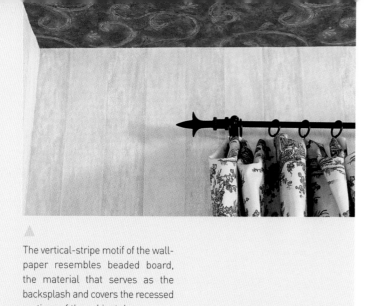

The vertical-stripe motif of the wall-paper resembles beaded board, the material that serves as the backsplash and covers the recessed portions of the cabinet doors.

GETTING THE LOOK: AGED CABINETS

The cabinets in this kitchen were once plain-panel birch in a natural finish. Beaded-board panels and an aged paint finish give the cabinets a fresh decorative look. To achieve a similar aged look for your cabinets, first remove the cabinet doors. Lightly sand the cabinets and doors; then prime and let dry. Paint with white or off-white paint; let dry. Mix 4 parts glaze to 1 part walnut stain and generously wipe onto the doors and cabinets, allowing the glaze/stain mixture to accumulate in the recessed areas of the panels. Oil-base (alkyd) products were used for this project, but water-base (latex) paints, stains, and glazes will produce equally impressive results. Water-base products are easier and safer to use than oil-base products, and they will not yellow over time as oil-base products tend to do. If you choose to use oil-base products for this or any project, carefully follow the manufacturer's instructions. For more information on distressing cabinets, see page 63.

MORE IDEAS FOR
Countertops

Countertops, usually noted for their functionality, have taken on new status as a kitchen focal point in recent years. Standard laminate, butcher-block, and ceramic tile countertops are readily available, but marble, granite, and stainless steel examples offer broader design possibilities. This exciting range of options allows you to choose the surface that best fits your decorating scheme and your normal cooking routine: Butcher block is great for cutting food; marble and granite make wonderful baking prep surfaces. Regardless of which you choose, keep in mind the cost of the material and its installation, the durability of the material, and ease of maintenance and cleanup.

This kitchen features three counter-top materials: butcher block, stainless steel, and granite.

Solid butcher-block countertops provide an ideal place for chopping vegetables, eliminating the need to soil a cutting board each time you prepare a salad. Made of hardwood strips, butcher block brings a sense of warmth to a kitchen, but it must be sealed for protection from moisture.

Most commonly associated with commercial kitchens, stainless steel has become a popular option in private residences. Besides being easy to clean, this material withstands the heat of pots and pans. Stainless steel is available in various finishes and treatments, from bright and mirrorlike to brushed or embossed.

Though expensive, granite is a beautiful and nearly indestructible counter surface. Ultracool and virtually stain-proof, it is perfect for rolling and kneading dough. To protect the surface, periodic application of a nontoxic penetrating sealant is required.

Concrete offers a tough, durable surface that withstands heat, but it stains easily. Because concrete can be tinted, it is at home in nearly any decorating scheme.

Marble countertops are a popular choice for baking and candy making because of their cool surface. This natural material is softer and more porous than granite and needs to be sealed like granite. Still, even when sealed, marble is less durable. The two materials are similar in price.

Streamlined for
LIVING

Open floor plans are wonderful for creating a sense of spaciousness, but blurring the line between a kitchen and a living area gives the kitchen decor added importance. Achieving the perfect blend of function and aesthetics is no small task. Here, a glaring fluorescent light fixture, black appliances, and visually heavy upper cabinets that have seen brighter days spoil the view from the adjacent family room. A well-considered remodeling added layers of charm while keeping all the function.

Work within the layout. In this transformation what stayed in place is as surprising as what moved: The stove, sink, dishwasher, and refrigerator all occupy the same spaces, leaving the basic layout and size of the room unchanged. However, with the upper cabinets and soffit removed and storage consolidated along one wall, the room looks and feels completely different. Two other elements are simply enhanced: A single metal window is replaced with two wood-frame windows, and the peninsula is lengthened and deepened to provide a larger work area that doubles as a casual eating area.

Re-evaluate the space. Next to the refrigerator a door leading to the dining room prohibited good use of the entire wall. Eliminating the door caused no inconvenience; an opening to the living and dining rooms is only a few feet down the wall, and it was enlarged to open up the floor plan even more. The result is a wall dedicated to storage needs—a desirable feature in any kitchen.

Visually expand the room. Along the same wall, a visual trick makes the room look larger: The cabinets closest to the living area are not as deep as the pantry cabinets, which are in turn less deep than the wraparound cabinet for the refrigerator. The staggered cabinets exaggerate the distance to the rear door, making the kitchen look grandly large.

Continued on page 74

BLENDING KITCHENS WITH LIVING AREAS

- Choose quiet appliances (especially dishwashers) and exhaust fans so that cooking and cleaning noises don't overwhelm the living area. Further, keep appliance colors muted; if possible, choose colors and finishes that blend with the cabinets or walls. Hidden dials and displays also make appliances less noticeable.
- Flow colors and styles between rooms. In this kitchen the flooring and white walls flow from one room to the other, making the transition to the living area seamless. Also consider the flow of window styles and coverings, light fixtures, and furniture styles.
- Add comfortable features to the kitchen, such as unfitted cabinets with the look of furniture and glass insets on upper cabinets for display areas. In this kitchen counter stools that look like chairs function perfectly and also seem at home from the living area.
- Nothing says "kitchen" more than a counter full of jars and other cooking accoutrements. For an open kitchen plan, be sure to include plenty of storage so utensils, cookware, and serving pieces are at hand but out of sight. Plan a spot for dirty dishes too; some homeowners add a second dishwasher so dirty dishware is never in view.

BEFORE

AFTER

To keep clutter off the countertops, tall drawers hold canisters and other bulky items.

AFTER

BEFORE

Warm the room with wood. With plenty of natural light and an overall white color scheme, both rooms are bright, but the warm wood floor and butcher-block countertops prevent the space from feeling cold. Beaded board covers the cabinets and walls for visual interest and adds a strong vertical element to the space.

Take the focus off the appliances. Every effort is made to reduce the visual prominence of appliances: The black-fronted stove and dishwasher are replaced with new white models, and the new stove has a downdraft feature, eliminating the need for a

hood. The microwave oven resides behind the pantry doors. To save money, the existing almond-color refrigerator is still in place, but new white cabinets that surround it minimize its visibility.

Consider flexible lighting options. Lighting an open kitchen can be a challenge: How do you get enough light without creating glare? Using a bank of recessed ceiling fixtures and adding dimmers will give you great flexibility; the lighting can be easily adjusted according to need.

Beaded-Board Paneling

You can buy tongue-and-groove beaded-board kits from a lumber supply or home improvement center. The wood comes in a variety of lengths and qualities: A higher-quality wood contains fewer knots, thus being easier to paint. Before purchasing beaded board, measure your walls carefully and consider which extras (for example, molding for baseboards) you may need to complete your project. Keep in mind that manufacturers recommend buying the paneling and bringing it indoors at least two weeks before attaching it to your wall. This gives it time to acclimate to the temperature of the room, so it won't shrink after installation.

The beaded-board paneling in this kitchen hangs directly from vertical studs and horizontal bracing. Find the position of the framing and mark it as a guide for nailing in the panels. Note that some kits contain clips for affixing the panels to the wall.

When applying beaded board, be sure the paneling is straight, or plumb. If the wall has any slope, you will need to trim the panel for a good fit so the piece will stand straight. Scribe the panel by holding it in its proper place and running a pencil down the wall so that the pencil marks a line that matches the slope of the wall. Cut the board along the marked line and nail in place.

You Will Need

Screwdriver or drill
Tape measure
Pencil
Beaded board
Saw
Carpenter's level
Hammer
6-penny finishing nails
Miter box (power or manual)

Molding, as desired
Surface compound, spackling knife
Optional: primer, semi-gloss enamel
   paint in the desired color,
   paintbrush
Optional: Water-base polyurethane

1. Remove all outlet covers, switchplates, and molding (including baseboards).

2. Cut the first piece of beaded board to the correct height for your particular project needs. Beginning in one corner, set the beaded board against the wall. Use a carpenter's level to check that it is perfectly straight and fits tightly against the corner. Nail the panel into place.

3. Continue around the room, keeping the top edge level at the height line until you have completed the entire wall surface. Cut the boards to special widths and lengths as needed to fit under windows and around doors. At corners, you can either overlap the boards or make miter cuts to join the boards at 45-degree angles (depending on the thickness of the paneling).

4. When the wall surface is complete, add molding for base boards and window trim, as desired.

5. Spackle over any knots in the wood and fill any nail holes; let dry.

Optional: If you don't want to leave the panel in its natural finish, prime and paint, allowing it to dry between applications. If the beaded board is in a kitchen or other room where it may need to be cleaned, apply a coat of polyurethane for protection.

MORE IDEAS FOR

Storage

Whether you spruce up your kitchen or completely remodel it, take some time to evaluate your current storage situation. Consider how and where food, cooking utensils, and small appliances are housed. Are related items grouped together? Are small appliances positioned close to the countertop where you use them? Do you keep the items you use most frequently near the front of a cabinet or drawer? Do you have space that isn't used as efficiently as it could be, for instance, a broom closet that could be converted into a pantry? Even if you believe you have ample storage, could you benefit from pullout shelves that make finding items easier? With a little planning, you can maximize your space to make cooking and other kitchen-related tasks more enjoyable.

✳ For hundreds of tips to help organize your kitchen, visit **HGTV.com/beforeandafterbook**

▶ Pullout shelves are a handy way to reach pots and pans and any items that may be stored near the back of the cabinet.

▲ A narrow slice of space on each side of a cooktop can be used to store slim items, such as spices and seasonings.

◀ Islands can accommodate full-size storage on one side and shallow shelves for spices, seasonings, and oils on the other. Some islands are open on one or both ends to allow storage and display space.

▲ A space-saving pullout pantry keeps supplies handy for cooking and blends in with the rest of the cabinetry when it is closed.

◀ This cabinet features a pullout shelf on the bottom and a pop-up shelf specially designed for a stand mixer. The mixer shelf eliminates the need to bring the heavy item up to the countertop for use.

Inviting
DINING

Sometimes starting with nothing is scary, because it's hard to know where to begin. It would have been easy to simply move into this dining room without addressing the worn carpeting or dull white walls, but by evaluating the space and uncovering an unseen gem, the homeowner brought the dining space beyond its humble beginnings to create a room with style and grace.

Work with the floor plan. Like many ranch-style homes with open floor plans, this home featured a long, narrow living and dining area with a low ceiling. The dark, uninspired space needed a boost. Warm taupe paint on the walls now makes the room inviting; a fresh coat of white paint overhead gives the ceiling a visual lift. Before, dingy carpeting concealed beautiful hardwood flooring. Now refinished, the floor provides visual warmth. A sisal rug, which brings in natural texture, protects the area beneath the table.

Define the spaces. Although the light colors helped visually widen and heighten the open space, the two areas still lacked definition. The solution is a movable wall that defines the living and dining areas and introduces a playful splash of orange in the mostly neutral space. This wall is shorter than the ceiling to make the room appear taller—and because the wall is only half the width of the room, the room seems wider.

Continued on page 80

BEFORE

AFTER

PHOTO FUN

Family photos become original artwork in this dining room. To create similar artwork, enlarge your chosen photos at a copy center and have them transferred to white canvas. **Note:** *In most cases, copy stores can make these types of canvases up to 3 feet wide and any length.* Sandwich the top and bottom edges of each canvas panel between pairs of 1x4s cut slightly longer than the canvas width and brushed with polyurethane. Screw the boards together. To hang, mount the bottom edge of the top board on nails driven into the wall.

Mix it up. The most essential feature in the room is the refinished round dining table. The table is covered with a tailored white tablecloth and surrounded by contemporary metal office chairs for a successful rendition of old-meets-new. A simple upholstered bench provides additional seating; its pipe legs complement the metal chairs and the legs of the divider wall.

A neutral backdrop is versatile. What makes this room so much fun are the splashes of color against the neutral background. The bright graphic pillows on the patterned bench and a green and blue Roman shade bring in cool tones that contrast nicely with the orange wall. A trio of family photos serves as bold, oversize artwork.

Freestanding Divider Wall

With basic woodworking skills, you can make a movable divider wall similar to this. This project will likely take a weekend to complete, but the result is worth the effort.

You Will Need

2x4s, cut two each of the following lengths: 69" (A); 48" (B); 16" (C); 45" (D)

¼-inch birch plywood, cut to the following dimensions: 3½x48" (E); 3½x72¼" (F); 3½x36" (G); 3½x15½" (H); 48½x71¼" (I)

No. 8x2½" deck screws

1" pipe flanges (2)

1"-diameter galvanized pipes (2), 40" long, threaded on both ends

Wood glue

6-penny finishing nails

1" galvanized pipe tees (2)

9" lengths of 1" galvanized pipe (4)

1" galvanized 90-degree pipe elbows (4)

Wood putty, putty knife

Primer, latex paint in the desired color and finish, paintbrush

Tape measure, pencil

Circular saw

Drill

Pipe wrench

Hammer

Jigsaw

Router with flush-trim bit

Handsaw

Sandpaper

Screwdriver

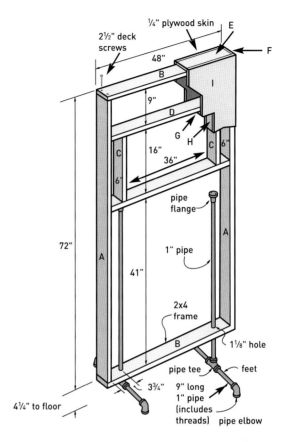

1 ■ Assemble the frame stiles (A) and rails (B) with 2½-inch screws. Position the window stiles (C) between the window rails (D) as shown in the illustration; attach with screws. Position the assembled window frame within the wall frame; screw into place.

2 ■ Attach two 1-inch pipe flanges to the underside of the lower window rail, centering one under each window stile. Drill two 1⅛-inch-diameter holes in the lower frame rail where shown. Insert the pipes through the holes, using a pipe wrench to tighten them into the flanges. (These pipes give the wall rigidity.)

3 ■ Attach the top and side frame skins (E and F) to the frame with glue and 6-penny finishing nails. Install the window rail skins (G) next, then the window stile skins (H).

4 ■ With a tape measure and pencil, mark the window opening on the panel skins (I); then use a jigsaw to cut about ¼ inch inside the lines. Apply a thin bead of wood glue to one side of the frame assembly, position one panel skin squarely on the frame, and nail the skin to the frame. Flip the frame over and attach the other skin in the same manner.

5 ■ Using a router with a flush-trim bit, trim the skin panels flush with the surface of the window frame skins. Carefully square the corners with a handsaw.

6 ■ Use a pipe wrench to assemble the pipe feet from tees, 1-inch pipe, and elbows, as in the illustration. Thread them onto the pipe extending from the lower frame rail.

7 ■ Fill any nail holes with putty, sand the surfaces smooth, and paint the wall with one coat of primer and two coats of paint, allowing the primer and paint to dry between coats.

MORE IDEAS FOR
Window Treatments

Window treatments can be more than a practical way to provide privacy, block glare on the television screen, and shelter you from the sun. They bring color, pattern, and texture into a room, carrying through the decorating scheme you have chosen. When preparing to purchase or create window treatments, consider the following: What is your style? Choose treatments and hardware that complement the mood you want to achieve (for instance, heavy velvet panels may have a place in a formal dining room but not in a cottage-style room). How is the room used? Do you need the treatments to block out the sun to protect artwork on the walls? If so, look for room-darkening treatments. Finally, consider the architecture of the space. Do the treatments need to hide flaws in the walls or windows or can the treatments show off these features? For extra style, use interesting curtain rods and finials to punctuate your overall scheme.

Valances—those little pieces of fabric that grace the top of a window—add softness, color, and pattern to a hard architectural element. These treatments are purely decorative, framing both the window and views. In rooms where privacy isn't a concern, valances may hang alone, but pairing them with shades, blinds, or panels offers privacy and more light control. The valances shown in this country-inspired kitchen are tab-top, with loops or "tabs" of fabric sewn into or onto the top seam.

Roller shades are an inexpensive window treatment option, but they often lack personality and style. This patchwork shade brings pattern and color into the room. The squares are arranged randomly for punches of color that aren't too predictable, but a precise checkerboard could also be created. A similar shade can be made with squares of paper-back silk ironed onto a standard shade.

Rod-pocket panels are a popular option because of their simplicity: The curtain rod simply slips through a channel (the pocket) sewn into the top edge of the panel. Often these panels are made of lightweight fabric and left unlined for a casual appearance. In this room ordinary panels gain interest and style with the addition of a contrasting fabric liner and trim.

Hinged to either side of a window frame interior, louvered shutters lend a fitted look to any setting. The slats can be opened and shut accordingly to your lighting, privacy, and ventilation needs. White is an ever-popular choice for shutters, but they are available in a multitude of colors and wood tones. These shutters provide a classic look; the crisp and clean appearance complements the summery blue and white scheme.

Fine DINING

The typical dining room plays a chameleonlike role in the house. The basic surroundings need to be interesting, and oftentimes elegant, but not express too much style. Rather, the mood and style of the dining event plays the lead. Creating that style can be quick and easy if you use items you already have on hand.

Start with the basics. Setting a fresh mood for any meal is an achievable goal; all it takes is a little planning. Start by creating a universal backdrop. In this dining area the pretty table and chairs, antique cupboard, and French doors are all a soft white. That makes the good lines of each element stand out when the room is not in use. A simple but elegant Italian art glass chandelier and an extensive selection of red and white transferware pieces keep the room pleasantly and adequately decorated even when the table isn't set. The red and white sets the tone for three different events: breakfast, brunch, and a formal dinner.

VERSION ONE: BREAKFAST

Keep it simple. For a casual breakfast, no tablecovering is necessary. The red and white plates help determine the choice of flowers: A pot of bright gerbera daisies set in a miniature gazebo creates a cheerful look with minimal effort. The vintage wood farm chairs have simple tied-on seat cushions with a skirt of old valance lace around three sides. Everyday meals provide added enjoyment when served in such pleasant surroundings.

Continued on page 86

VERSION ONE: BREAKFAST

VERSION TWO: BRUNCH

VERSION TWO: BRUNCH

Dressed up but not stuffy. For a slightly more formal Sunday brunch (shown on page 85), three square tablecloths create a colorful geometric pattern that's much more interesting than a single tablecloth. If company is coming for the meal, set aside the everyday (in this case, transferware from the cabinet) and bring out something special (in this case, white ironware). Slipcovered parsons chairs sit at either end of the table to add to the dressed-up look of the room. The centerpiece is a classic cement bust ringed with ivy and topped with a garden cloche, bringing a touch of the outdoors to the room.

VERSION THREE: DINNER

Pull out all the stops. The most formal occasions call for the most refined dinnerware and decor. In this dining area the good silver is put on display in the cabinet, adding gleam and shine to the space. The curl-top parsons chairs show their elegant green Jacquard upholstery. And the table is topped with layers of lace tablecloths and filmy fabrics. The best china with gold rims is mixed with antique teacups to create a unique place setting for each guest. The centerpiece only looks expensive: It's a candy dish topped with a glass vase; together they display flowers (set in florist's foam) and a candle.

Slipcovers allow the same chair to be dressed for completely different occasions. This dining chair has a lace-trim cushion for casual affairs and a more elaborate cover with dressmaker details for special events.

CUSTOM SLIPCOVERS

Slipcovers are becoming more readily available in various styles, but you may prefer a custom slipcover for that special chair or sofa. One of the most cost-effective ways to have slipcovers made, or to have any custom sewing work done, is to find a good workroom. Firms are often listed under Upholstery or Drapery in the Yellow Pages, but the best source is word of mouth. Ask friends for the names of firms they've used. You're looking for someone who knows the ins and outs of working with textiles and furniture. Expensive fabric may make you swoon, but if it isn't expertly sewn, it will be a disappointment. These skills are so much in demand that some of the best workrooms do work only for interior designers. If you find a workroom through the Yellow Pages or a similar source, have the shop make a pillow first so you can check the quality of the work. Get the specifics written down and agreed upon before the work starts, as you would for any professional service, and stay in touch with the workroom throughout the project to ensure the work is progressing on schedule and on budget.

VERSION THREE: DINNER

SERVING UP STYLE

To create beautiful settings quickly and conveniently, you'll need key elements on hand. Start by picturing the kinds of meals you plan to serve.

- **Begin with breakfast.** If your dining room is in use daily, start by gathering the items you'll need for family meals. A good, sturdy table that can handle constant use is a must. Here, the painted table and chairs have good lines, but they're basic pieces that won't suffer from a few dings and nicks. Tableware, too, needs to be sturdy. In this house a collection of red and white transferware is at the ready in the cabinet. The pieces are complementary, not matching, and most are vintage. A few chips or the loss of a piece won't upset the balance.

- **Plan for regular events.** Casual entertaining calls for a second layer of decorating. Here, the better china, the slipcovers for chairs, and the tablecloths are all of the same caliber and well-suited to each other. Have more than you need for any one occasion if you entertain regularly to give you the flexibility to create a variety of settings. If you have these special second-level items on hand, it will take no time at all to make Sunday dinner, birthday gatherings, and relaxed entertaining even more special.

- **Be ready for formal only if you'll really do formal.** There's no point in having formal dinner service for 12 if you'll use it only once a year. If, however, you don't have good china and a big event is coming, consider renting the good stuff. It may be expensive, but the cost is a fraction of what you'd pay to buy and store good china and silver for the rare use. If you entertain frequently, keep the good china and linens easily accessible so you'll use them often.

- **Use a little creative thinking.** Repurposed candy dishes, layered linens, and mix-and-match dishware all contribute to a dining area with interest and charm. As you collect favorite items, consider how they can be used; gather and group enough of them to adequately cover the table.

- **Plan the table when you plan the meal.** If you're planning to entertain, imagine how you want the table to look. That way, if there's something you've been longing to add to your collection or something that needs replacing, you can address the need ahead of time, not at the last minute. Once table planning becomes habit, you'll do it without stress. A little think time also allows you to experiment with ideas just for fun.

Slipcovers

If you have dated, dingy furniture in need of rescue—or if your living spaces could benefit from some fresh color and fabrics—slipcovers may be the solution. Slipcovers let you introduce new style into any space, and slipcovering is much more affordable than reupholstering. Outdated or tattered upholstery disappears when topped with a pretty slipcover. Heavily patterned winter fabrics can give way to refreshing whites and light prints for summer. Perhaps best of all, if you have mismatched furnishings, slipcovers can unify the pieces.

Even the simplest of chairs can take on a whole new look with a slipcover. This tailored example in a summery fabric is dressy enough for a formal gathering yet still looks comfortable and inviting.

Delicate rose embellishments and dressy piping detail this slipcover. The full skirt, reminiscent of a flowing ball gown, is a classy touch.

If the thought of making a slipcover is daunting and you can't find the right ready-made for your particular chair, think of other ways to dress it up. This once-tired chair sports a fresh coat of paint; a flanged pillow and tufted seat cushion add comfort.

SLIPCOVER BASICS

- When making or purchasing slipcovers, choose low-maintenance fabrics that can be machine-washed with ease.
- Look beyond current furnishings for slipcovering potential: Old chairs with simple lines are an easy fit and an inexpensive option.
- Before purchasing, check the sturdiness of any old furnishings you select for slipcovering. Also check that the old upholstery is clean, so that old stains won't show through the new fabric.
- If your chosen chair isn't comfortable, cut new foam for the cushion and wrap it with batting for extra loft.
- Add details, such as piping, fringe, rope, or braiding to customize a ready-made slipcover.

Simply CHARMING

Sometimes it's the quick, inexpensive changes that transform a space. In this dining area adding fabrics and expanding the colorful plate collection make the space more inviting. This is a great example of using what you have—in this case, the dining set, a grouping of plates, and pleasing paint colors on the wall and wainscoting—as the basis for a fresh take on a room.

Give a collection purpose. To create a focal point with lots of impact, two plates are added, and the grouping is rearranged in an arched fashion. The walls of this room are tall, and the pale yellow visually expands the space even more, so additional plates make the collection more effective. The new bright green and blue plates provide a punch of color against the cheerful walls.

Use fabric to unify the space. The dark-stained dining set looked out of place against the crisp white wainscoting and yellow walls. To tie the table and chairs to the other elements in the space, coordinating blue and white plaid fabrics are introduced in a tablecloth and new drop-in seat covers. The seat covers replace a predominantly dark green plaid that made the chairs look outdated.

QUICK AND EASY TABLECLOTH

Even if you don't own a sewing machine you can easily create a tablecloth for a square or rectangular table. Choose a fabric in a color and motif that coordinates with other elements in the room. Wash and dry the fabric to remove any sizing; iron. Cut the fabric into the desired shape and size for your table, adding a $\frac{1}{4}$- or $\frac{1}{2}$-inch seam allowance to each side. A drop of 8 inches is recommended (it won't drape onto diners seated at the table). Following the manufacturer's directions, use $\frac{1}{4}$- or $\frac{1}{2}$-inch-wide fusible hem tape to finish the edges of the cloth.

❋ For more simple tablecloth ideas, visit **HGTV.com/beforeandafterbook**

BEFORE

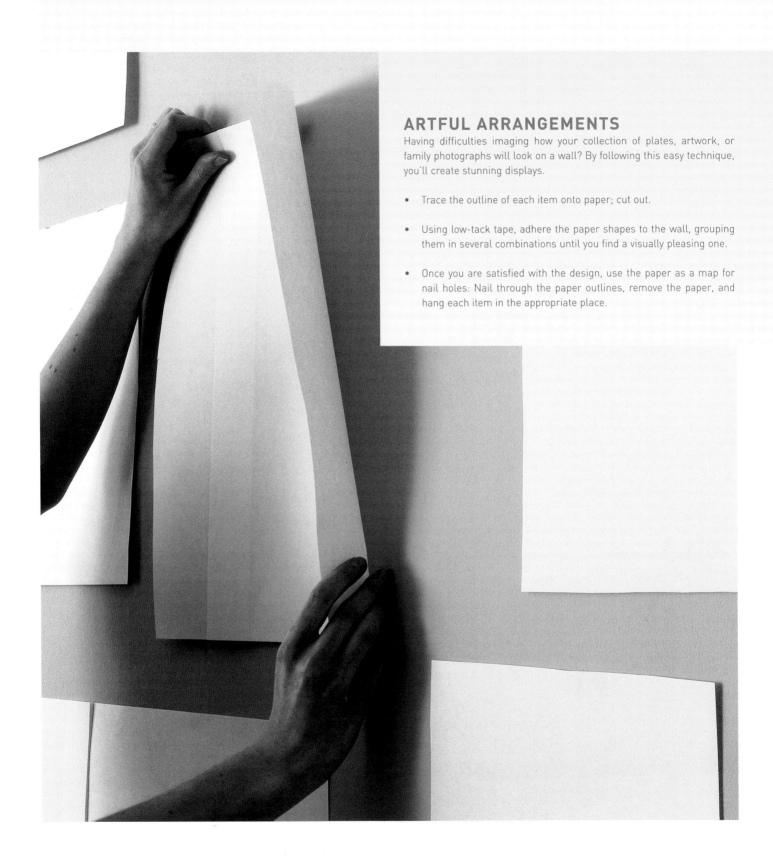

ARTFUL ARRANGEMENTS

Having difficulties imaging how your collection of plates, artwork, or family photographs will look on a wall? By following this easy technique, you'll create stunning displays.

- Trace the outline of each item onto paper; cut out.

- Using low-tack tape, adhere the paper shapes to the wall, grouping them in several combinations until you find a visually pleasing one.

- Once you are satisfied with the design, use the paper as a map for nail holes: Nail through the paper outlines, remove the paper, and hang each item in the appropriate place.

Drop-In Seats

Consider the power of fabric in dining areas: The addition of a tablecloth and new drop-in dining chair seats in a coordinating fabric can introduce much needed doses of color and pattern. Re-covering old, worn drop-in seats is a quick way to freshen dining chairs. For this project, select a fabric with a tight weave that can stand up to stretching; choose one that is lightweight so it won't add bulk to the seat and make it difficult to fit into the frame.

You Will Need

Screwdrivers, flat and phillips
Fabric in the desired color and motif
Pins
Scissors

Optional: high-density upholstery
    foam and polyester batting in
    desired loft, sized to fit seat
Optional: spray adhesive
Staple gun, staples

Remove the seat from the chair, using a screwdriver if necessary.

Using the flat screwdriver, carefully remove the staples that hold the fabric to the seat. Use caution; you will use the old fabric as a pattern.

Lay the new fabric flat, right side down. Place the old fabric on the new fabric; pin in place and cut around the edge of the old fabric.

If the old foam and batting are flat and stained, replace them with new high-density foam and polyester batting. Adhere the foam to the wood seat with spray adhesive; top with the batting.

With the fabric right side down, center the foam- and batting-covered seat on the fabric, foam side down. Starting on one side, pull the fabric to the underside of the wood seat and staple in the center. Repeat on the remaining sides, pulling the fabric taut. Continue stapling around the fabric until it is secured. At the corners, neatly fold and staple. After stapling is complete, trim any excess fabric.

Replace the seat in the chair.

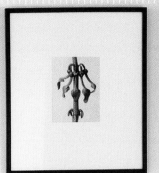

Arranging Wall Art

Arranging artwork on your walls can be one of the more daunting decorating tasks you face—but it doesn't have to be. Here are some basic rules to follow the next time you want to do an arrangement. Generally, place artwork at eye level, giving consideration to the piece you're hanging and who will be viewing it. In a child's room, for example, place the piece at his or her eye level for easy viewing. Choosing the right hardware to hang your pieces is important. Use picture hooks that can withstand the weight of your pieces, and consider decorative hangers, such as drawer pulls, that go beyond their intended function. Choose frames and mats that enhance the artwork: If you have simple art, treat it to a decorative frame; let elaborate art stand out by giving it a modest mat and frame.

Grouping like objects creates drama; these four pansy watercolors lend an airy, arty mood to this space. Consistency in framing ties the paintings together, and the symmetry of the arrangement creates a more formal look.

Artwork can be a strong focal point when matted and framed in the same manner and arranged symmetrically. This series of photos hangs above a sofa; a similar arrangement would work above a long table or buffet in a dining room.

Pictures don't always have to be hung in a row; frames don't have to match. This interesting arrangement pairs illustrations in different sizes and frames with a few ornate mirrors. The stimulating grouping keeps the eye moving.

A Matter of COLOR

Introducing fresh, strong color. Rethinking furniture placement. Balancing furnishings and accessories. Creating a focal point. Blending a television with its surroundings. These are the keys to making this combination dining/sitting room more functional, cozy, and comfortable. If you have a space with similar needs, use this room as a guide for your makeover.

Behold the power of paint. What was once a sterile, uninspired place is now enveloped in warm color. The striking red complements the dark wood table and the plaid furnishings and window treatments. It also brings out the best in the accessories, including prints of guinea fowl. The new color defines all these elements and makes them stand out even more.

Find a focal point. Because the furnishings were small and out of scale with each other, the dining portion of the room lacked a clear focal point. A corner armoire replaces the small dresser that held the TV—and becomes an instant focal point. Treated to a distressed paint finish in black and dark brown, the armoire holds a smaller television, as well as a collection of porcelain dishware, vases, and bowls. To accommodate the electrical cords from the TV, a hole is drilled in the back of the armoire. To best display the collections and television, the doors on the armoire are always open. Because the door fronts are more attractive than the backs, the doors are reversed so that the fronts face outward into the room.

Balance and proportion are key. Four prints hung in a grid pattern balance the armoire and add rich gold color against the red walls. The large platter that hung above the table finds a new home on the opposite wall, beneath a wall-mounted display cabinet, where its size is more appropriate. The dresser that served as the TV stand now sits between the two chairs in the sitting area, providing additional space for displays and beverages.

Make room for diners. At the table, taller Windsor chairs look better—and are much more comfortable for diners—than the old short barrel chairs. The table has grown by a leaf and stands parallel to the wall, allowing diners to sit all around it instead of three sides only.

Continued on page 98

BEFORE

AFTER

BEFORE

AFTER

Comfort for two. Initially, only one ottoman served the sitting area, and it typically held a tray for snacks and coffee. Now, two ottomans allow a pair to put up their feet while watching TV. The ottomans can also serve as extra seating if necessary.

Look beyond the intended use. The new floor covering is actually a fringed tapestry tablecloth, which was given a pad backing to prevent it from slipping.

CHOOSING PAINT COLORS

Paint is undoubtedly one of the easiest, least expensive ways to make a dramatic impact in any room. If you are ready to bring color into your home but are unsure of how to evaluate colors before making a commitment, use painted sample boards to audition your selections. Prime a piece of foam-core board. Use a board that has the same texture as your wall, because textured surfaces will appear darker than smooth surfaces painted the same color. Paint the board, allowing it to dry completely (paint usually looks darker dry than when it's wet). Move the sample board around the room, observing how it appears in different light, from morning to night and near different light sources. Notice how the color interacts with furnishings, artwork, and accessories in the room. When selecting paint for this exercise, keep in mind that the sheen, or finish, will also affect appearance. Flat paint will look darker than semi-gloss, and semi-gloss will look darker than gloss (the shinier the paint, the lighter it will appear).

MORE IDEAS FOR

Focal Points

Living rooms are where most people consciously set out to create a focal point. However, any room that is used for sitting and conversation needs a focus, an item or area that draws the eye and unifies the furnishings. In living rooms, fireplaces, large picture windows, and pieces of art are obvious candidates for focal points; in dining areas, the same items can be the focus. In addition, impressive pieces of furniture, such as armoires, china cabinets, and buffets, can command attention and anchor the space.

Artwork can be a dramatic focal point, as this contemporary piece demonstrates. The spindle-back chairs, which originally had cane seats, are upholstered in red to complement the painting.

Fireplaces are a typical focal point in living rooms, but how about in a dining room? To create ambience around this table, a salvaged antique fireplace mantel is mounted on the wall. A crackle finish gives the mantel an old-time feel, and an upholstered bench tucked into the firebox transforms the mantel into a banquette.

The focal point of this Swedish-style dining room is made up of two pieces that appear as one unit: a painted sideboard and a plate rack.

Customized screens are an inexpensive way to bring interest to a room. This focal point screen is painted with blocks and swirls of color and has cutouts that display a sponged wall treatment behind it.

BEDROOMS

Tiny to TERRIFIC

At first glance, design oddities detract from this small bedroom in a 1950s ranch, but smart design strategies turn them into unique opportunities. Paint and tailored Roman shades unify the windows; a headboard becomes a fitting focal point and adds storage space; light-color berber replaces old commercial-grade carpet; and—voilá—this room is now as comfortable as it is classy.

Unify with paint. The horizontal row of louvered windows set high in the wall is spaced unevenly, and one window had been replaced with an air-conditioning unit that created an eyesore. Rather than camouflage the home's midcentury roots, the homeowner emphasized the horizontal nature of the windows by painting a stripe on the walls between the windows (thus turning the windows and wall sections between them into one sleek unit). Now the eye notices the windows without noticing they are off-center. The soft layered design of the Roman shades adds subtle horizontal lines, which accent the painted stripe. The space with the air-conditioner is treated like the other windows; the shade is left down when the unit is not in use.

Emphasize the focal point. The feature attraction is the new headboard, which fits neatly under the high windows. The headboard design incorporates two built-in side tables, offering a place to stash reading materials, an alarm clock, and matching lamps. The outer edge is trimmed with black, and the interior is padded with a dark gray flannel. The black and gray, blue walls, white trim, and multicolor bed linens make for a crisp, masculine look.

Continued on page 106

BEFORE

AFTER

AFTER

Ordinary doors can have design flair. French doors leading to a small office create an offbeat look. The stiles separating the 15 glass panes are boxy, without a routed edge, and the bottom edge of the doors is no wider than the top. Now painted in the same black as the headboard, the doors are drawn into the overall design of the room. Translucent film (available at home improvement centers) covers the glass panes, so these once odd doors now resemble a shoji screen. This adds a contemporary edge that complements the look of the room.

Padded Storage Headboard

This headboard—intended for use with a queen-size bed—is constructed of plywood and medium-density fiberboard (MDF), with padded squares of foam-core board as the interior. The back of the unit is made from a full sheet of sturdy plywood. MDF, which has a clean, paintable edge, makes up the two end tables. MDF is quite heavy; consider having it cut at a home improvement center so the pieces are easier to handle.

You Will Need

4x8' sheet of ¾" MDF cut to the
   following: 4'x14" (2); 12x16" (4);
   6x12" (4)
4x8' sheet of plywood
15' 1x2
6 penny nails
1¼" wood screws
4x8' sheets of foam core (2)
Polyester batting

3 yards decorator fabric in the desired
   color and motif, 45" wide
Spray adhesive
Packing tape
Construction adhesive
Utility knife, scissors
Drill
Primer, latex paint, black and color
   that coordinates with wall
   color, paintbrush

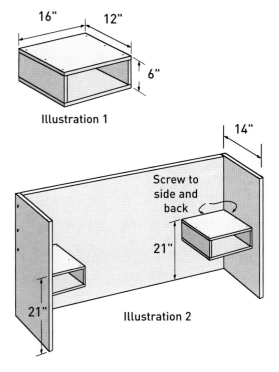

16"   12"   6"

Illustration 1

14"

Screw to side and back

21"

21"

Illustration 2

1 ▲ Attach the 4-foot-by-14-inch pieces of MDF to the sides of the plywood. This creates the headboard unit.

2 ▲ Following the illustration, make two side tables with the four 12x16-inch pieces and four 6x12-inch pieces of MDF, gluing and then nailing the pieces together. (Illustration 1) Note that the front and back of the tables will be open.

3 ▲ Attach the two side tables to the headboard unit with screws. Position the top edge of the tables 21 inches above the bottom of the unit. (Illustration 2)

4 ▲ Cut and adhere 1x2 to the side and top edges of the headboard.

5 ▲ Prime the entire unit; let dry. Paint the interior and inward-facing 1x2 edges black. Paint the top and sides of the unit in a coordinating color; let dry.

6 ▲ Determine where you will need to run electrical cords through the back of the unit (near the side tables). Drill holes where desired.

7 ▲ Cut 16 of the following for the back of the unit: 15-inch squares of foam-core board, 16-inch squares of batting, and 17-inch squares of fabric. Cut 4 of the following for the sides of the unit: 12½x13-inch pieces of foam-core board, 13½x14-inch pieces of batting, and 13½x15-inch pieces of fabric. Spray each piece of foam-core board with spray adhesive; wrap batting around the board. Spray the batting with spray adhesive; wrap the fabric around the batting-covered board. Trim any excess batting and fabric; use packing tape to secure the edges, if needed.

8 ▲ Starting at the top of the unit, glue the 15-inch-square batting- and fabric-covered pieces of foam core to the back wall of the unit. Glue six squares across to form the top two rows; glue four squares in the bottom row, between the two side tables. Glue two 13x15-inch batting- and fabric-covered pieces to each of the sidewalls, above the side tables.

❋ For more do-it-yourself headboard projects, visit **HGTV.com/beforeandafterbook**

Headboards

Beds are often the focal point of a bedroom, but they can't reach this status with bedding and pillows alone. To truly make your bed take center stage, consider adding a headboard. Any of these ideas can be implemented in an afternoon, but keep other options in mind too, such as a folding screen with fabric panels that complements your bedding or an artist's canvas the width of your bed covered with fabric or paint accents. If your bed already has a headboard, find ways to emphasize it, for example, with a fabric slipcover.

Ordinary fence pickets can add cottage charm to any bedroom. To construct a similar headboard, use pickets of different lengths; this example uses 11 pickets cut into graduated lengths, from 50 inches (the tallest middle piece) to 34 inches (the shortest end pieces). Two cross boards are bolted to the pickets, one 1 inch from the bottom and the other 27 inches from the bottom. For a similar weathered look, prime the headboard unit and paint two coats, sanding between coats. Attach the unit to the wall or bed frame using drywall screws or anchor bolts.

Bring the outdoors into your bedroom with a bright floral headboard. These fun flowers are painted freehand on a piece of plywood with various colors of acrylic paints and artists' paintbrushes; then, the outline of each flower is carefully cut out with a saw. To complete the headboard, the cut edges of the motifs are painted, and then the unit is attach to the bed frame (the bed shown has a low headboard with posts).

Decorating doesn't get any easier than this: Old tin tiles lined up behind a bed provide instant vintage charm. If you have difficulty finding antique tiles at flea markets or antiques shops, look for reproduction tiles at home improvement centers or crafts stores.

Vintage textiles are sometimes too fragile to use as bedcoverings, such as this 1837 quilt, but they make beautiful faux headboards. Displayed vertically, the pieced quilt makes the walls appear taller than they are.

This stylish headboard treatment puts soft gusseted pillows to work as decorative accents. For a similar look, choose three coordinating seat cushions with ties already attached and add them to a window treatment rod mounted above your bed.

Traditional RETREAT

A bedroom should be a retreat, a private oasis from the rest of the world. This bedroom had all the basics in place—a comfortable, high-quality bed, a makeup table, and an easy chair—but the dominant blues of the large Oriental rug and painted walls created a chilly feeling.

Temper strong color with pattern. The bright blue rug, with peach and terra-cotta accents, needed to stay in place to warm the hardwood floors, but finding appropriate wallcoverings and fabrics to complement the rug required careful planning: The rug needed strong elements and strong colors to balance it. A pretty blue and white trellis-pattern wallpaper and predominantly red floral fabrics—used for the romantic bed draperies, bed skirt, and window treatments—introduce a jolt of color and add vertical lines to offset the horizontal "weight" of the rug.

Window treatments can emphasize—or disguise. Fabrics play an important role throughout the room. The old window treatment was a simple valance and louvered shutters. The new treatment has full-length panels with blue-check trim and a valance for a fuller, more finished look. The unusual round window over the bed posed an interesting challenge. Instead of following the arc of the window, the treatment covers the entire section of wall behind the bed; stationary lace sheers stretch between the two bed drapery panels.

Unify the elements with fabric and color. The chairs in front of the window, once covered in a striped fabric, are now upholstered in neutral beige that blends with the other furnishings in the room. Another chair sits at the makeup table; its drop-in seat features the same blue-check fabric that appears in accents throughout the room, visually connecting the elements.

Choose one item to bring it all together. To tie together all the elements in the room—the Oriental rug, trellis-print wallpaper, neutral bed coverlet and upholstered chairs, and floral and checked fabrics—a bright patchwork quilt is placed at the end of the bed. This simple accessory unifies the room, acting like a visual bridge for all the colors to come together.

BEFORE

AFTER

This window treatment features floral and checked fabrics.

MIXING PATTERNS SUCCESSFULLY

Keep the following points in mind when incorporating different patterns in a room.

- **Limit the color palette.** In this bedroom, red is the dominant force, but touches of blue and white link the soft furnishings, the wallpaper, and the rug.
- **Consider scale.** Varying the size of the patterns adds interest, but keep the size of the room in mind too. Large patterns will overpower a small space but look at home in bigger rooms; small patterns won't have impact in large areas but are perfect for little spaces.
- **Keep it simple.** Introduce a limited number of patterns: Sticking to three—for instance, a floral, stripe, and plaid—adds interest to a room without overwhelming the eye.
- **Balance the patterns.** Distributing patterns throughout a room will make for a smooth transition; positioning them together in groups, or clumps, creates too many focal points.

PROJECT

Wallpaper Like a Pro

Wallpaper choices are almost limitless: Hundreds of patterns in a myriad of colors to suit nearly every decorating style are available. Wallpapering an entire room may seem daunting, but with planning, forethought, and patience, you can dramatically change the look of the room.

Before choosing a wallcovering, consider your experience level, the features of the room, and the look you want to create. Some papers, such as stripes, are easier for beginners to hang because there is no pattern to match. However, stripes can be hard to hang straight on crooked walls and will accentuate flaws in the wall surface. Papers with floral designs require matching, but the busyness of the design often disguises flaws in the hanging or in the walls.

You Will Need

Wallpaper primer
Chalk line
Scissors
Wallpaper
Water tray
Optional: wallpaper paste

Wallpaper brush
Damp cloth or sponge
Straightedge
Razor knife with several extra blades
Seam roller

1 Clean the wall and cover it with a primer designed for wallcovering applications. To help conceal any small gaps in seams, tint the primer to match the wallcovering background. The primer seals the wall, helps the wallpaper bond better, and creates a surface with good "slide," making the wallpaper easier to manipulate for pattern matching.

2 Choose an inconspicuous corner—for instance, behind a door, where pattern mismatching will be least obvious—for a starting point. Snap a chalk line to mark a straight vertical line on the wall. This line indicates a true vertical. Establish another true vertical line when you turn a corner or start a new wall.

3 Cut the first strip of wallpaper 6 inches longer than the section of the wall you're covering to allow for trimming. For prepasted wallpaper, roll the strip, print side up, and immerse it in a tray filled with water. Let the paper soak for the time specified in the manufacturer's directions. Unroll the paper and lay the strip on a clean, washable surface, paste side up. If you are using wallpaper that isn't prepasted, don't soak it in water; instead apply paste to the dry wallpaper. "Book" the strip by loosely folding—but not creasing—both ends to the middle; this keeps the paste from touching the front of the paper. Let the strip sit for the time indicated by the manufacturer; this allows the paste to activate and the paper to expand and contract.

4 Hang the first strip by unfolding the top end (leave the bottom end folded for the time being), holding it up by the corners, and lining it up with the chalk line. Allow 3 inches of wallpaper to overlap the top edge, for trimming. Unfold the bottom half of the strip and continue to align it with the vertical chalk line. Allow the bottom 3 inches of the strip to overhang for trimming.

5 Smooth out wrinkles and bubbles using a soft brush and sweeping movements. Use this technique for each strip as you hang it: Start at the top middle of each strip and work the brush diagonally to the right. Go back to the top middle and brush to the left so your motions form a triangle. Sponge off any wet paste that seeps from the edges to the front of the paper.

6 Continue applying successive strips, aligning the pattern and smoothing the covering.

7 Trim any excess wallpaper from the top and bottom edges, using a straightedge and sharp razor knife. Change the blade frequently to avoid tearing the paper. Trim each strip while the paste is still damp; then flatten the seams gently but firmly with a seam roller. Sponge off any wet paste that seeps from the edges to the front of the paper.

8 To paper around doors and windows, cut a rough opening with 3 extra inches on all sides from the dry strip that extends over the door or window opening. Moisten the strip and hang it. Make diagonal cuts near the corners of the opening. Smooth the paper around the frame; trim, then clean with a damp sponge.

9 To wallpaper around outlets and light switches, turn off the electricity to the outlets and remove the covers. Position the wallcovering over the outlet or switch opening, cut an X with a razor knife over the opening, and smooth the paper into place. Trim the four flaps made by the X. When you are finished, reattach the covers and turn on the electricity.

WALLPAPERING TIPS, TRICKS, AND TECHNIQUES

- Fix wall damage, such as cracks, flaking paint, and holes, before priming and hanging wallpaper.
- To avoid mildew growth, prime walls with a mildew-proof wallpaper primer before papering.
- When trying to match a pattern, peel back the paper and reposition it. Overworking the paper can stretch it.
- Press gently on the seam roller. Otherwise, you may force out too much paste and cause curling at the seams.
- Use only high-quality washable paints near wallpapered surfaces, because paste smears can be difficult, if not impossible, to remove from unwashable paint.
- Apply wallcoverings in normal room temperature and humidity conditions. Extreme heat and humidity can cause drying problems.
- Use good lighting to ensure a quality application.

MORE IDEAS FOR

Canopies

If your bedroom lacks charm, consider surrounding your bed with a canopy, which will create an instant focal point. Even if you don't have a canopy bed, luxury and romance can be yours if you install some hardware and a fabric that complements your decorating scheme.

Lightweight scrim provides a gauzy cover when strung through two chrome-finish brass towel rings attached to the ceiling.

Four-poster beds can look charming with canopies, but draping fabric all around may be cumbersome and look too childlike. For a stylish solution, hang one panel at the head of the bed; this treatment softens the space and gives the appearance of a headboard.

In this charming bedroom, four wrought-iron rods, forming the main rectangle of the canopy, hang from the ceiling. A blue and white check cotton fabric is tied between the rods, and floor-length panels are tied in the same manner. Brass finials provide a finishing touch in the corners.

This bedroom looks like a romantic bed-and-breakfast retreat, thanks to vintage linens and cottage decor. Fabric hung from a J hook in the ceiling drapes over unused swing-arm lamps flanking the bed, creating a lovely canopy.

Hand-Me-Downs
Get DRESSED UP

Is your bedroom filled with dissimilar furnishings or lack cohesion? Many homeowners are often faced with a mismatched group of furnishings and hand-me-downs from family members and friends. Such was the case in this bedroom. The young home-owners had a nice queen-size bed and functional storage pieces, but the window treatments were different, and there were no nightstands on which to set an alarm clock or reading lamp. Rearranging the room, restyling the mismatched pieces for unity, and adding Mediterranean-inspired colors made the room into a welcoming oasis from everyday stress.

Let the bed take center stage. First, the bed is moved closer to the window. To make the bed a more suitable focal point, it is set at a slight angle for a commanding presence, and a shutter screen serves as a makeshift headboard (the actual headboard is low). The screen also helps channel the heat from a heating vent near the bed. Slipcovers in muted beige, green, and red cover the headboard and footboard. These colors set the stage for an inviting room that is bathed in soft colors and textures and natural finishes.

Dual window treatments are versatile. The old, mismatched window treatments give way to bamboo window shutters and rice paper shades that are versatile enough to let in ample light during the day and block out streetlights at night. The horizontal lines of the shutters and folding screen are a nice visual contrast to the strong vertical pattern on the head- and footboard slipcovers.

Mix and match storage pieces and furnishings for visual interest. A dark-stained dresser and white cubes provided ample storage space opposite the bed, but they weren't unified. The storage cubes are moved to the closet, where they stack on the existing closet shelf and organize sweaters and little-used

clothing. The dresser wears a fresh coat of white paint to help lighten the main space. Additional storage enters the room in the form of a blanket chest at the foot of the bed. The mix of white-painted furnishings and molding and natural woven elements—the bamboo shutters, the nightstands, the wicker blanket chest and chair—is inviting rather than distracting.

Continued on page 118

BEFORE

AFTER

AFTER

BEFORE

Carve out comfort. With the storage cubes moved to the closet, a vacant corner becomes an intimate reading nook where a chandelier hangs above a comfortable chair. The room lacks overhead lights, so this fixture brings in much-needed general lighting. Additional lighting also comes from petite lamps with beaded-fringe shades, which occupy the new nightstands.

Anchor the space with color and texture. To complete the makeover, the dingy carpeting is replaced with hardwood flooring, which has been painted white. The white flooring combined with the beige walls and white ceiling creates an airy space. An area rug beside the bed ushers in additional textures and color.

Bamboo Shutters

In this bedroom, a dual window treatment effectively lets in light and provides privacy. A white rice paper shade plays a supporting role, but the homemade bamboo shutters are the real attraction. With basic woodworking skills and easy-to-find materials you can create these shutters. The instructions are for making one shutter; repeat the process for a pair.

You Will Need

Tape measure
Wood trim
Sander or sandpaper and tack cloth
Radial arm saw
Bamboo sheets
Latex paint in the desired color and finish, paintbrush
Small nails
Hammer
Optional: wood glue
6 L-brackets, screws
Nail set
Wood filler
Router
Cabinet hinges
Shade to fit window dimensions

1. Measure the window around the frame interior where you will attach the hinges. Cut two pieces of wood trim to fit the height measurement (lateral pieces) and three pieces of wood cross members to fit between the two longer pieces. Sand the wood pieces; remove dust with the tack cloth.

2. On one edge of the lateral pieces create a slot by ripping to a ½-inch depth, ¼ inch wide (two blade kerfs) or slightly wider than the bamboo.

3. Cut the cross members (horizontal pieces) in half thickwise so you have six narrow pieces that will be placed back-to-back over the bamboo.

4. Cut the bamboo to size, allowing for the width of the cross member as well as the depth of the slots. The slots will be used to hold the material in place.

5. Paint the wood pieces; let dry.

6. Nail the cross members together, sandwiching the bamboo between. For more stability, glue these pieces together. Slide the bamboo into the slot of one lateral piece until the lateral piece meets the cross member at the top corner. Place an

L-bracket at this corner and screw on to stabilize the corner. Nail the cross members onto the shade as you did the top. Place an L-bracket at the bottom corner and screw on.

7. Place the two center cross members on the middle of the shutter, one on the back and one on the front; nail together. Place an L-bracket on the corner where the lateral piece and the cross member meet; screw on.

8. Slide the second lateral piece onto the remaining edge of the bamboo until the top of the piece meets the top cross member. Place an L-bracket at the top, middle, and bottom corners where the cross members meet the second lateral piece; screw on.

9. Use a nail set to countersink small nails into the cross members. Fill in the holes with wood filler.

10. Rout pockets in the finished shade on the side that will be hung on the window frame. The hinges will sit in these pockets.

11. Touch up over the wood filler and L-brackets with paint; let dry. **Note:** *To completely cover the L-brackets. use several coats.*

12. Affix the hinges to the window frame to hang the shutters.

Screens

Folding screens—constructed of everything from wood to metal and embellished with papers, ribbons, photographs, and hand painting—add something special to almost any room. These versatile design elements can set off a cozy corner for reading, hide clutter, or create architectural dimension in a blank square space. Ready-made screens are plentiful and easily personalized. If you can't find a premade screen you like, make one from bifold closet doors, louvered panels, or even a garden trellis.

The colors, patterns, and textures of Asian design take center stage in this bedroom. Behind a stream-lined, diagonally set Art Deco bed stands a dark wood screen with a hand-painted ginkgo leaf design.

Colorful paper cutouts resembling origami shapes are combined with rice paper and a clean-lined frame to create a screen with Asian flair. Rather than block light, this tall screen diffuses it through panels fitted with rice paper and chicken wire.

Bifold closet doors, available at home improvement centers, can easily be made into a screen with two-way hinges. This screen is covered with wallpaper and topped with a coordinating border. Ribbons tacked to the top of the doors hold framed artwork.

A playfully hand-painted screen set in the corner of this formal bedroom provides a much needed break from the expanse of blue walls.

Colorize, TEXTURIZE

A great bedroom starts with a great bed. The bed is where you sleep, relax, and read; it's also most often the focal point of the room. Give your bed the status it deserves with stacks of pillows and cozy bedding, and surround it with furnishings and accessories that complement rather than detract from it.

This bedroom had a lot going for it, including a beautiful wrought-iron bed and coordinating full-length oval mirror. However, the pale lavender walls—while restful—were lifeless, and the cotton bedding, gauzy bed skirt, wood nightstand, and unadorned paper chandelier shades were void of much-needed pattern, color, and texture.

Punch up the scheme with fresh color and textures. To take this room up a notch on the style chart, a warmer shade of lavender paint now covers the walls, and bright, cheery colors make their entrance via pillows made of woven satin ribbons and a coordinating suite of projects: a chandelier, nightstand topper, and flowing bed skirt. These accessories not only bring in color, but they also set the stage for new textures, which can both be seen and felt. Textures also make their way into this cheerful space via a soft chenille throw and a green Jacquard duvet cover.

Use artwork to unify. Matted and framed artwork is added to one wall to break up the expanse of lavender. This piece of art brings together all the colors now present in the room.

RIBBON BED SKIRT

Creating a custom bed skirt is quick and easy with a flat sheet, ribbons, and fusible hem tape. Cut a flat sheet to fit the box spring, allowing an extra ¾ inch at the foot end and sides. Hem the edges. Measure from the top of the box spring to the floor and cut ribbons of the same length in various colors to attach to the sides and foot end of the sheet. (In this example, 1½-inch-wide ribbons in six colors are used.) Using a wood-burning tool as described on page 124 to cut the ribbons will prevent the ends from fraying. Cut fusible hem tape to the length of each side and the foot end; remove the paper and temporarily adhere to the sheet edges. Press the ribbons to the tape and iron, following the manufacturer's instructions.

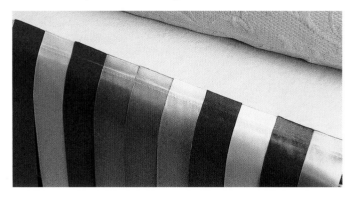

BEFORE

AFTER

Woven Ribbon Pillow

Satiny soft pillows made of interwoven ribbons are a luxurious place to rest your head. These instructions are for two colors of ribbon, but choose as many colors as you desire to complement your decor.

You Will Need

Scissors, crafts knife
Foam-core board
Tape measure
1½" wide single-face satin ribbon, two colors
Straight pins

Fusible interfacing, iron
Fabric for pillow back (i.e., cotton or satin)
Sewing machine, needle, matching thread
20" pillow insert

1 ▪ Cut the foam core to a 22-inch square with the crafts knife.

2 ▪ Cut 28 ribbons, 14 of each color, each 21 inches long.

3 ▪ Line the ribbons of one color in a row on the foam-core board, with the shiny side down. Allow no gaps between the ribbons. Secure each end of the ribbon strips with straight pins.

4 ▪ Beginning with one piece of the remaining color of ribbon, secure one end to the foam core with a straight pin, shiny side down. Weave the ribbon through the ribbons placed in Step 3, going over and under the ribbons. When complete, secure with a straight pin. Repeat this process with the remaining ribbons, alternating the ribbon weave to create a checkerboard pattern.

5 ▪ After the entire panel is woven, adjust any ribbons that are not tightly secured in the weave.

6 ▪ Cut a 21-inch-square piece of fusible interfacing. Iron the fusible interfacing to the woven ribbons, following the manufacturer's instructions and removing pins as you iron. Discard the foam core.

7 ▪ From the backing fabric cut a 21-inch square. With the right side of the fabric and shiny side of the ribbon unit together and a ½-inch seam allowance, stitch three of the sides together. Turn right side out, insert the pillow form, and whipstitch the opening closed.

USING A WOOD-BURNING TOOL

To prevent ribbon ends from fraying, use a wood-burning tool to cut the ribbons. Use caution when working with a wood-burning tool, because it will be very hot. Also note that you will need a nonmelting cutting surface and a metal ruler for cutting straight edges.

Woven Nightstand Top

This fun table topper is a great way to spruce up a nightstand. An ornate iron plant stand was used for this example, but this versatile design will work equally well on any standard wood nightstand or other tabletop.

You Will Need
Tape measure
Foam-core board
Scissors, crafts knife
Nightstand
1½"-wide single-face satin ribbon, two or more colors
Fusible interfacing, iron
Straight pins
2 pieces of ⅛"-thick framing glass, cut to size of nightstand top with the edges sanded

1. Measure the edges of the nightstand top and add 2 inches to each measurement. Using a crafts knife, cut the foam core to match these measurements.

2. Cut as many 1½-inch-wide ribbons as needed to cover the length and width of the foam-core board. If using two colors, cut equal amounts of each color; if using more than two colors, cut as many of each color as desired.

3. Follow Steps 3 to 6 for the Woven Ribbon Pillow, cutting the fusible interfacing to size (1 inch smaller than the foam-core board).

4. Sandwich the woven ribbon panel between the two pieces of glass. Place the completed topper on the nightstand.

Woven Chandelier

Lampshades are available in every shape, size, and color imaginable, but few are as pretty as this. This chandelier has an ordinary paper shade, metal rings at top and bottom for structure, and a hanging cord. Similar inexpensive fixtures can be found at home decorating and discount stores.

You Will Need
Hanging lamp kit
Tape measure
Scissors
1½"-wide single-face satin ribbon, two or more colors
Low-temperature hot-glue gun and nonflammable glue sticks

1. Assemble the lamp, following the manufacturer's instructions.

2. Measure the circumference of the shade and the length from top to bottom (from metal ring to metal ring).

3. Cut as many ribbons as required to cover the circumference of the shade in the desired colors. If using two colors, cut equal amounts of each color; if using more than two colors, cut as many of each color as desired. Set aside.

4. Cut as many ribbons as required to cover the length of the shade in the desired colors. If using two colors, cut equal amounts of each color; if using more than two colors, cut as many of each color as desired. Set aside.

5. Adhere the circumference ribbon ends to the shade in a row, shiny side up, aligning the seams at the back of the shade. Allow no gaps between the ribbons.

6. Beginning with one piece of the length ribbon, adhere one end to the shade at the top (near the metal ring). Weave the ribbon through the ribbons placed in Step 5, going over and under the ribbons. When complete, secure the end at the bottom metal ring with hot glue. Repeat this process with the remaining ribbons, alternating the ribbon weave to create a checkerboard pattern.

Pillows

Pillows are one of the most versatile decorating accessories around. They can be purchased or made in nearly every shape, size, color, and fabric motif imaginable, to complement the decor of every room of the home. Better yet, they are easy to personalize with any number of details, from trims and fringe to appliqués and buttons. Take pillows beyond the bedroom: In large sizes they can serve as seating in family rooms; smaller cushion-type pillows add comfort to dining room chairs.

❋ For more pillow projects you can make, visit **HGTV.com/beforeandafterbook**

Outgrown shirts make a fun, tailored addition to this bedroom; customized pillows and a pieced and quilted bedspread dress the bed for success. Pillows similar to these can be easily constructed from one shirt or many shirts when they are cut and pieced together. When cutting old shirts to make pillows, quilts, and other projects, use the tailored features, such as plackets, cuffs, and pockets, as interesting details instead of only using the larger areas of shirt fabric.

Ribbons, rickrack, fabric scraps, and ready-made appliqué flowers combine in a sweet, country-inspired pillow. Embellish a purchased pillow cover in a similar fashion by first stitching "stems" of ribbon or rickrack onto the pillow front. Cut floral shapes from scrap fabrics and appliqué them over the stems. To complete the look, attach an appliqué shape, such as a flower or circle, to the center of each flower, using fabric glue or by hand-stitching.

Fleece is one of the easiest, most forgiving fabrics for sewing and crafts projects. It doesn't fray, which means you don't have to be concerned with raw edges. This cozy square pillow features four equal-size squares on its front. To create a similar pillow, cut two 13½-inch squares (for the pillow front and back) from one color of fleece; cut four squares or other shapes from a contrasting color. Glue the small shapes to the pillow front; use perle cotton and a large-eye needle to create a running stitch around the shapes. Put the pillow front and back right sides together and stitch three sides, using a ½-inch seam allowance. Turn right side out, insert a pillow form, and hand-stitch the opening closed.

Good As GOLD

If you entertain overnight guests and you are lucky enough to have a designated space to accommodate them, consider the room a guest getaway. When planning a guest room space, imagine yourself in the guest's position. When you are a guest in someone's home, what amenities do you prefer? A television? Places to sit and relax? This guest room had a comfortable queen-size bed, plenty of natural light for daytime activities, a beautiful refinished hardwood floor, and a place to stash clothing and personal items. The overall neutral palette, while restful, was uninspired. It took some paint and French-style accents to make this room a warm, inviting space.

Wake it up with paint. The most obvious difference in this makeover is the paint color. When selecting a paint color, it is often easiest to use what's in the room—furnishings, flooring, accessories—as inspiration. In this room, however, the opposite occurred: The homeowner chose paint colors to audition, then decorated around the chosen color (see page 98). A vivid yellow-orange won the lead part and now enlivens the room. Fortunately, the homeowner remembered a piece of French crewel in cream, gold, and brown, dating from the mid-1800s, at a local antiques store. Although the piece is only large enough to cover a twin-size bed, it provides the mix of color and texture the space needed.

Layer in softness. To make the bed an interesting focal point, textiles are layered on top of it. The crewel is the top layer. Below, a piece of cream-color antique linen visually lengthens the crewel, and the original taupe bed skirt adds a tailored finish. Two large pillows are covered in old linens and a grain sack, providing additional texture and old-world charm.

Layers also appear on the windows: The long drapery is tied back with hemp twine, and another piece of antique linen serves as a long valance. Combined, the two neutral-color pieces of fabric let in light while providing the privacy that guests require.

Continued on page 131

BEFORE

AFTER

AFTER

BEFORE

The next time you are expecting overnight guests, have these items on hand—or similar items that cater to the preferences of your guest (for instance, a CD player and CDs your teenage niece enjoys).

- Bedside light and clock
- Extra pillows, blankets, and fresh linens
- Bottle or carafe of water and glasses, electric kettle and tea bags or other beverage service, and a fruit basket
- Reading materials, writing paper, and a pen
- Mirror
- Comfortable chair
- Clean towels and washcloths and travel-size toiletries
- Clothes hangers and a place to stash luggage
- Flowers

Use neutral hues and wood tones to tone down bold color. Although the new, energizing color dominates the space, it is neutralized by the crisp white moldings, freshly painted dresser, and touches of silver throughout. Silver—seen in the bedside lamp and accessories, curtain rod, and dresser hardware—acts almost like an ice cube, cooling down the space. The wood floor now glows in the presence of the bold walls, but the warm tone of the wood also neutralizes the space.

Refresh tired furnishings. The dark-stained dresser, a hand-me-down that served as an entertainment center, was too dominating. To soften its harsh appearance it got a coat of white paint, which complements the molding; the original pulls are painted silver. Now the dresser does more than serve as storage space: The TV is gone, and a much needed mirror and stylish topiaries grace the dresser top.

Complete the look with elegant accessories. To round out the room, the once bare walls display a white platter and two elegant French-inspired wall sconces, featuring curved lines and drop crystals for a spark of romance. The new bedside table—which took the place of a chair—has ample space for a reading lamp, a clock, and other bedroom necessities.

THE GREAT PAINT EXPERIMENT

Painting colors directly on a wall will give you the most accurate indication of how a color will appear. You can also use primed sample boards, as described on page 98, and move them around the room to see how the colors change throughout the day in different lighting conditions.

MORE IDEAS FOR

Guest Rooms

When planning a room for your overnight guests, keep your own wish list in mind. When you are away from home, do you like a place to lounge while reading the morning paper or a fresh robe you can slip into after a shower? To see if your guests will be comfortable, sleep in the space yourself. If you don't have a special room to dedicate to guests, consider underused areas, like lofts or basements; or temporarily convert a den or office into a guest haven with a movable screen.

Complete with romantic netting, this "napping couch" invites guests to drift off to sleep in the summer breeze. If it's too chilly at night, the door at far right leads to the main house, where other sleeping quarters can be found.

What used to be a workshop is now a guesthouse that opens to a patio. Painted finishes on an open-beam ceiling, plywood walls, and a concrete floor dress up the space, which is filled with flea market finds.

A little-used loft space can be the perfect hideaway for guests—and a place you can use as a get-away-from-it-all retreat when you don't have overnight visitors.

This room is filled with everything a guest could desire in a home-away-from-home, including a table for primping or writing notes, a comfortable place to enjoy a cup of tea, and an inviting bed with mounds of pillows.

Room for TWO

It is not uncommon for children to share rooms when they are young and receive separate spaces as they grow older. In this case, however, two boys who once had their own rooms—but usually ended up sleeping in each other's rooms—now share a space that inspires fun and creativity.

A loft saves space—and offers more than a place to sleep. Sleeping quarters were addressed first. The existing full-size bed stays in place, but to conserve space a custom loft is constructed above it to hold another mattress. The ends of the loft structure are open storage and display space—an important feature for a room that contains possessions of two instead of one.

Storage for two. To further tackle storage needs, each child has his own red-painted dresser, and the closet is divided into two separate areas. Bins and hanging storage (shown on page 136) allow plenty of space for clothing, footwear, and sports gear. The dressers face each other, creating a designated changing area.

Continued on page 136

GROWTH CHART

This growth chart resembles a football field—a nod to the favorite sport of the two boys. The chart is painted on a wall that was first coated with magnetic paint; the footballs are homemade magnets that can be moved as the children grow. Nearly any motif can be used—including animals, musical notes, and racecars—to suit your child's interests.

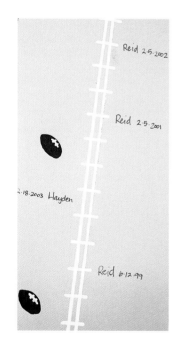

Reid 2.5.2002

Reid 2.5.2001

2.18.2003 Hayden

Reid 6.12.99

BEFORE

AFTER

Stacked bins and hanging storage create plenty of space for two boys' possessions.

AFTER

BEFORE

ROOMS THAT GROW

When planning a room for your child or children, keep an eye on the future. When you purchase versatile furnishings, select a lasting color scheme and choose enduring design motifs so the room will grow with your child. Use these cues as a starting point for creating a safe, comfortable haven your child will enjoy for years to come.

- When planning a nursery, select a crib that converts into a toddler's daybed. Often, the bedding can be used for both, saving you money. This also makes the child's transition from crib to bed easier.
- Look beyond traditional kid colors, such as blue for boys and pink for girls. Gender-neutral colors, such as reds, greens, and yellows, can create a timeless look.
- Avoid trendy motifs, such as the latest cartoon character, that your child will quickly outgrow. To appease your child, incorporate these motifs through inexpensive, easy-to-change accessories, including throw pillows, lampshades, and photo frames.
- Theme decorating often makes selecting fabrics and accessories easy, but choose themes that have stood the test of time, such as floral, nautical, and Americana motifs.
- When selecting fabrics, opt for easy-care cottons in geometrics, stripes, florals, and solids that can be easily mixed and matched.
- If planning a room two children will share, consider current and future needs (for instance, play spaces when they are young and study spaces as they grow older). Create a room where each child has space for his or her possessions and provide common areas where lessons on compromise and sharing can be learned.

Bold color and graphic motifs bring excitement. The room was originally painted a soft yellow, with bright furnishings, bedding, and accessories. This color scheme was invigorating, but there was no real style theme. The room required a more sophisticated scheme that could grow with the boys. The new color and design scheme is inspired by contemporary striped fabrics in white, brown, and red, found on the new chair and ottomans, and fun red circle mobiles hung by the windows. Stripes and dots—both reminiscent of sports symbols—are now present throughout the space, on the custom duvet covers and pillows, wall art painted by the residents, and storage containers. A crisp stripe treatment is even painted below the window. A neutral light brown paint on the walls allows the shapes and bold red to take center stage.

Personalize with paint. To encourage creative play and display, sections of the wall and dressers are covered with magnetic paint, providing a surface on which to showcase favorite photographs and artwork. Homemade magnets in letters and sports motifs can be moved from surface to surface with ease.

Time for rest. Finally, to give the children a spot to sit, relax, and read a book with Mom or Dad, a comfy chair now sits beneath a large window, which features a scallop-shape valance and brown Roman shades. Ottomans provide a place for the boys to put up their feet and can be used for extra seating.

PROJECT

Dressed-Up Dresser

Dressers serve an important purpose in a bedroom—storage on the inside and display space on top—but why not make a dresser a place for fun too? This dresser has both cork and magnetic surfaces for kids to tack up pictures and mementos. Magnetic paint is readily available at crafts stores and home improvement centers; most often, it can be covered with paint in any color for a truly personalized look. To dress up the magnetic surface, create custom magnets.

You Will Need
Dresser
Sandpaper, tack cloth
Primer
Paintbrushes
Magnetic paint
Latex enamel paint in the desired
   color and finish
Tacky glue
Cork squares
Crafts knife
Scissors
Jumbo rickrack

1 ▦ Remove the drawers and any doors from the dresser. Lightly sand the dresser, drawers, and doors; remove dust with the tack cloth. Prime; let dry.

2 ▦ Select areas to be painted with magnetic paint; on this dresser, the sides and back are painted. Paint the desired areas, following the manufacturer's instructions; let dry.

3 ▦ Paint the entire dresser the desired color of latex enamel paint; let dry.

4 ▦ Using tacky glue, adhere cork squares to the top portion of the dresser back. If necessary, cut the squares with a crafts knife to fit the width of the dresser.

5 ▦ Cut jumbo rickrack to serve as a border for the cork section. Adhere to the cork with tacky glue.

MORE IDEAS FOR

Kids' Rooms

Children's rooms are some of the most fun to decorate: They are a great place to experiment with color, pattern, interesting paint treatments, and even furniture arrangement. When decorating a child's room keep safety foremost in your mind; among other items, always choose child-safe paints as well as beds that meet current safety standards. After safety, aim for enduring style. Selecting versatile furnishings—for instance, a crib that converts into a toddler bed—and a lasting color scheme not dependent on a new, popular superhero will help you create a room that will grow with your child. The rooms shown here are decorated in a primary color scheme, but pastels, jewel tones, or even neutrals may also convey a child's interests and personality.

Select colors, motifs, and furnishings that can grow with your child. The look of this room can easily mature through the conversion of bunk beds into side-by-side twins, a change of bedding, and the removal of the throw rugs. Ample storage that is easily within reach of a child is a key to a well-functioning room. This room features built-in shelving as well as a tall cupboard that resembles an athletic locker.

Clean and uncluttered, this young child's room features headboard shelves that store and display toys and tic-tac-toe pieces; platform beds offer extra storage. The clean white framework will coordinate with any decor as the child grows older and develops different tastes. Bright fabrics and accessories in primary colors, accompanied by geometric patterns, look crisp against the white walls and furniture.

For lasting style, choose a theme that isn't too childlike. The nautical look of this room makes it appealing for a child of any age. Washable 100-percent-cotton fabrics in a bold check motif, chambray blue walls, and white-painted furnishings contribute to the timeless feel of the room.

From Country Cousin to CITY SOPHISTICATE

A common decorating mistake is to fill a room with too much of a favorite thing. In this case, the bed and bath were too cute and too pink: pink walls, pink floors, and pink textiles. Every accent was dated, over-the-top country. With no contrast and no established focal points, the rooms felt visually adrift.

Use color as the starting point. An about-face gave the bedroom the balance it needed. The color scheme—a neutral camel beige with black accents—is the foundation for the new look. The walls and floors are similar shades of honey-beige; the carpet is a textured berber with a hearty look and feel. Furniture in dark tones adds needed contrast.

Window treatments can do more than block sunlight. New window treatments also add texture and color. The old drawn-back panels make way for honey-tone bamboo Roman shades that are mounted outside the window molding to visually maximize the size of the window and control light and privacy. Layered on top are sailcloth panels attached by silver ring clips to brushed-silver rods. The rods are hung almost at the ceiling, and the panels hang to the floor, another design trick to accent the height and size of a window.

Continued on page 142

ACCENTING IS EVERYTHING

When a room gets a complete overhaul, be prepared to change everything. In this room it's difficult to imagine anything coming forward unchanged; only the dresser's classic lines saved it from going to the resale shop.

- **Lamps.** The rounded pink lamps are replaced with a slender, brushed-nickel lamp with a translucent shade next to the bed and a classic urn-shape lamp on the dresser. Mixing, rather than matching, makes the room more visually interesting

- **Side chair.** Next to the bedside table, a light and airy wicker chair replaces a pink rocker. The wicker's texture adds depth and contrast while continuing the warm, natural tones in the room.

- **Wall art.** A pink and blue heart-motif quilt hung above the bed; aside from the color scheme, it is much too childlike for an adult's bedroom. The matted architectural bridge drawing is not only more appropriate, but it adds a nice horizontal element to balance the bed's strong vertical lines.

- **Bedding.** In this room the new bedding is not only appropriate for the redo, but the layering makes the bed much more inviting and pleasing to look at: beige sheets, an off-white cotton blanket, a wool camel-hair blanket, and a stack of pillows.

- **Tabletop accessories.** Every picture frame, basket, and vase is new to the space. The new room simply couldn't accommodate any of the style of the old room.

BEFORE

AFTER

BEFORE

Splurge on style. The old bed was the only item with no redeeming style qualities. Now a slatted mahogany bed that stands taller resides in the room, along with a nightstand of the same style. Two black leather bedside footstools complement the deep, rich wood.

If it still functions—and has good lines—salvage it. An old dresser had nice lines but a bad finish and an unappealing three-panel mirror. Clunky hardware and stain that exaggerated the wood grain gave way to a smooth black satin paint finish and simple silver hardware. Now the curving lines of the piece rightly dominate in cool dramatic fashion. A simple black-frame mirror rests casually on the dresser top. Polishing the look of the old dresser helped it fit in with the new furniture.

If you don't need it, pitch it. The second tall dresser shared the same good lines, but crowded the small room, which has two large closets. In its place a tall tropical plant fans out to fill the space, adding a natural touch.

ARTFUL ADDITIONS

Improved printing processes and readily available standard-size picture frames have made adding wall art to any room easier and less expensive than ever before. In a streamlined setting like this suite, using one simple frame style in similar sizes throughout creates cohesiveness. For personalized artwork similar to that shown here, purchase standard-size frames with precut mats. Even if the mat doesn't have exactly the right size of opening, it may be close enough to fit or you may be able to re-create the photo. By scanning the image—either at home or at a drugstore or copy center—and printing it on photographic paper, you can resize it to fit whatever frame you choose. You can also adjust the color (heightening or muting the tones) to better suit a room. In this master suite black and white photos provide a fitting graphic look.

The long window treatments are hung close to the ceiling ▶ to emphasize the height and size of the window.

AFTER

The master bath shared the same unfortunate look as the bedroom, with the additional dismay of a visually vibrating pink sponge treatment on all the walls. The floor was not spared; it sported pink heart-motif linoleum. The wood tones offered no visual relief; there was a plethora of poorly grained wood.

Unify two spaces with compatible colors. To revive this space, the same style modus operandi is employed: Wash the room with warm tones and accent with black. The walls were sanded down to remove the residual texture from the sponge painting; then they were painted a neutral honey-beige two tones darker than the bedroom. Painting adjoining rooms the same basic color but a touch lighter or darker adds enough contrast to link and separate the spaces. The same goes for the window treatments: In the bedroom bamboo shades and full-length curtain panels in cream are used; a complementary cream-color Roman shade with a custom ribbon edge covers the bathroom window.

CUSTOMIZING PURCHASED SHADES

A band of black grosgrain ribbon adds punch to plain shades. For a similar look, iron the shade flat to make it easier to attach the ribbon. Cut the ribbon to fit about 1 inch inside the edge of each side. Carefully attach the ribbon with fabric glue or fusible hem tape, following the manufacturer's instructions.

BEFORE

AFTER

A brushed-nickel faucet complements the new cabinetry hardware.

Ceramic floor tiles are an easy-clean option in a bath.

Brushed nickel lends a sophisticated feel. A brushed-nickel, two-handle faucet gives the plain white oval sink a fresh new look. The vanity and storage cabinet have the same black paint covering and brushed-nickel hardware as the bedroom dresser. New towel bars also sport a brushed-nickel finish. Over the vanity, a new four-light fixture with ribbed, frosted-glass shades provides plenty of light. Replacing the wood toilet seat with plain white, a minimal expense, makes it less noticeable.

Tiles are a smart flooring choice. In this bath redo, the biggest expense is new flooring: Creamy white tiles in 4x4 squares now cover the floor. Designers often disagree on whether a small bath should have small or large tiles, so choose which you prefer. The key is in the grout color; match the grout to the tile to blend rather than contrast, and the space is bound to look bigger. Of course, the light color choice helps too. A small sisal rug is the perfect accent for this floor.

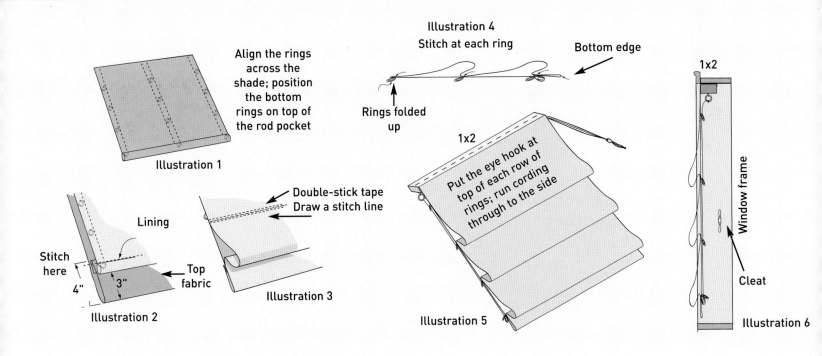

Align the rings across the shade; position the bottom rings on top of the rod pocket

Illustration 1

Illustration 4
Stitch at each ring

Bottom edge

Rings folded up

Stitch here

Lining

4"   3"

Top fabric

Illustration 2

Double-stick tape
Draw a stitch line

Illustration 3

1x2

Put the eye hook at top of each row of rings; run cording through to the side

Illustration 5

1x2

Window frame

Cleat

Illustration 6

PROJECT

Roman Shades

Roman shades, a classic window treatment, are actually quite easy to make. Despite the simple construction, ready- or custom-made Roman shades will cost you—far more than the materials for this project. The shades are made so that the top fabric hangs in folds; the lining hangs straight, and the top is stitched to the lining across the width of the shade at each ring. The overhanging fabric hides the stitching.

You Will Need

Tape measure
1x2*
Table saw
Scissors
Lining fabric*
Decorator fabric, in the desired color and motif*
Rings
Sewing machine
Double-stick tape
Disappearing-ink marker
Staple gun, staples
Eye hooks
Cording*
Cleats
1½" wood screws, screwdriver
¼" metal rod
*Measure window prior to purchasing and cutting materials

1. Cut the 1x2 one-half inch shorter than the window width.

2. Cut the lining fabric ¼ inch shorter than the window width and the same as the window height. This allows 1 inch at the bottom for a rod pocket and 2 inches at the top to attach the shade. Finish the raw edges and fold over the bottom 1 inch to form a rod pocket; stitch.

3. Cut the decorator fabric ½ inch wider than the window width and 48 inches longer than the window height. Finish the raw edges. Fold over the bottom 4 inches to form a rod pocket; stitch.

4. Starting at the bottom edge of the lining, right side up, evenly space three rings across the lining width. Continue spacing rings across the lining, placing them 5 inches apart along the length of the lining. (Illustration 1)

5. Place the lining right side up on top of the decorator fabric, also right side up, aligning the rod pockets. Stitch the lining to the decorator fabric where the rod pockets meet. There will be 3 inches of decorator fabric exposed at the bottom. (Illustration 2) Fold the joined lining and fabric so that the front of the lining faces the back of the decorator fabric.

6. With the lining on the bottom, fold 10 inches of the decorator fabric to align with the row of rings above the lining rod pocket. Fold the rings up so that you will not stitch over them. Using double-stick tape, temporarily adhere the lining to the decorator fabric right above the line of rings. If desired, draw a stitch line with the disappearing-ink marker, right below the line of rings. (Illustration 3) Stitch.

7. Repeat Step 6, folding 10 inches of decorator fabric to align with the additional rows of rings. (Illustration 4)

8. Staple the remaining top 2 inches of decorator fabric to the 1x2. Attach three eye hooks to the 1x2, aligning them with the three rings spaced across the width of the fabric. For the left-hand and middle cords, cut lengths 2 times the window length plus the width. For the right-hand cord, cut a cord half that length. Tie one end of each cord to the ring at the bottom (near the rod pockets). Thread the cords through each loop in the corresponding column and run them all through the right-hand eye hook. (Illustration 5)

9. Secure the cleat to the right-hand side of the window frame with screws.

10. Attach the 1x2 to the window frame with the 1½-inch wood screws. (Illustration 6)

11. Put the metal rod through the rod pocket.

Unifying a Bedroom and Bath

If your bedroom/bathroom suite doesn't feel like a unified space, use the following tips to create flow between them. First, consider color of paint, wallcoverings, fabrics, and even flooring and decorative accessories. Choose dominant and accent colors that work well in both spaces, regardless of their architectural features. Besides being perfect places to display color, fabrics used as window treatments, slipcovers, and bedding are a great way to bring complementary patterns and motifs into the bedroom and bath. Next, notice the surfaces and finishes that appear in each room: If you have a marble-top vanity, consider adding marble-top or marble-accented bedside tables. Finally, use accessories, including artwork and collections, to forge a link between the spaces.

A taupe and white color scheme—and graceful decorating—unifies this bedroom and bath. In the bath the white fixtures, tile, and cabinetry create a sense of spaciousness. The taupe and white wallpaper adds warmth to the light that streams in from the windows. Additional color in the bedroom—green plants, pink flowers—blend well with the taupe and white theme. The architectural piece above the bed recalls the bathroom wallpaper pattern.

The colors, textures, and imagery of the sea combine to create a bedroom and bath filled with a sun, sea, and surf atmosphere. In the bathroom light pours in through a large tub window; the breezy blue and white palette found throughout, including the glazed ceramic tiles, captures the colors of ocean waves. The bedroom, complete with a round window that resembles a porthole, shares the maritime atmosphere of the bath and boasts an impressive view.

BATHROOMS

Cottage-Style RETREAT

A bathroom needs to be functional, but that doesn't mean it can't be a beautiful, soothing space where you can escape from daily stress. Before this bathroom was treated to fresh fabrics, an inviting color scheme, charming beaded-board panel, and friendlier lighting and storage, it was a sterile, unwelcoming space. Devoid of charm, the room featured dry-walled walls, bare-bulb lighting centered over small medicine cabinets, and pedestal sinks with narrow rims that barely accommodated soap and toothbrushes. Further, storage was an issue: Wire shelving near the sinks held toiletries and other bath essentials but looked cluttered.

Emphasize the assets. The focal point of this bathroom, the beautiful claw-foot tub, set the stage for the makeover: The vintage look and feel served as the inspiration for the new cottage style. The tub is too large to remove—and too expensive to replace—

BLANK-SLATE DECORATING

If you have an all-white room with little personality—and it doesn't function the way you want it to—here are some ways to jump-start the makeover process:

- **Evaluate what works and what doesn't.** Do you have enough space for the activities you do in the room? Is there ample storage and lighting? Does your room have great architectural features you want to play up? Thinking about the good (and how you can play it up) and the bad (and how to remove or restyle it) is the right place to start.

- **Consider your budget.** It's important to prioritize and decide what changes you can make to get the most bang for the buck. The tub in this bath would have been difficult to remove and expensive to replace. With new reproduction hardware and a few coats of special epoxy paint to spiff up the porcelain, the tub looks good as new. Keeping the tub left money for fresh fabrics, wallcoverings, and even new wall-mounted sinks.

- **Get inspired.** Do you love a particular color or decorating style but haven't had the opportunity to try it yet? Is there an element in the room, for instance, an outside view or architectural detail, that can drive the decorating? In this room, the paneled door and vintage claw-foot tub lent themselves to a cottage style. If you aren't sure where to begin, review collections of coordinated wallcoverings and fabrics, which take the guesswork out of choosing.

- **Address the details.** The little things, such as new hardware and light fixtures, can provide major style. Often, these details are inexpensive but their decorative impact is significant.

but it required a makeover of its own. With a few coats of specially formulated epoxy paint to refresh the tired porcelain, and a coat of soft green paint on the outside, the tub regains its charm and status. Reproduction brass hardware and a pretty shower curtain accent the new look. A spindle-back chair provides seating—and serves as a makeshift table for towels and reading materials during long, relaxing baths.

Coordinated fabrics and wallcoverings unify. Fabric and color play a big role in this bath: Floral and striped fabrics in cream, green, and pastel pink provide visual and real softness in the shower curtain, valances, sink skirts, and chair cushion. A coordinating wallpaper and rickrack border continue the cottage-style scheme above the newly installed beaded-board panel and on the storage chest.
Continued on page 152

BEFORE

Store in style. Storage was a problem in this bath, but the newly decorated space handles it with grace. The once dark, grungy chest is now a pretty place to store toiletries and display personal items. The chest is painted the same soft green as the tub and treated to decoupaged cutouts from a coordinated wallcovering. Pleated sink skirts hide bathroom necessities; exposed storage above the toilet (not shown) holds towels, toiletries, and collectibles. Even the ledge above the beaded-board panel gets in on the act, serving as a display shelf for accessories.

Consider function and aesthetics. The original pedestal sinks, while functional, are replaced with wall-hung sinks, which have wider rims for holding everyday items. Above, the old-fashioned medicine cabinets carry the vintage feel one step further, and vintage-style light fixtures provide a polished alternative to the harsh bare bulbs.

SINK SKIRTS

Sink skirts are a charming—and functional—addition to any pedestal or wall-hung sink. Besides providing color and pattern to coordinate with other fabrics in the room, they can hide essentials such as tissues, toiletries, and cleaning paraphernalia. The pleated skirts featured in this bathroom are attached to the sinks with hook-and-loop tape, making them easy to remove for washing.

To make a simple gathered version, measure around the sink or vanity from wall to wall; multiply the measurement by 3 to allow enough fabric for pleating. Measure the height of the sink or vanity from where you plan to hang the skirt down to the floor; add 3 inches to allow for top and bottom hems (a wide hem adds body and weight to the bottom of the skirt). Sew a 2-inch bottom hem and a 1-inch top hem. To pleat the skirt, use a toothpick to push equal amounts of fabric beneath the sewing machine foot and stitch across 1/4- to 1/2-inch-wide pleats. Stitch one pleat at a time and then use the toothpick to push through more fabric. Cover the pleating stitches with jumbo rickrack, braiding, cord, or ribbon. Attach the skirt to the sink or vanity with hook-and-loop tape.

BEFORE

Decoupaged Chest

Dressing up a tired piece of furniture—or a new unfinished piece—is easier than you might think with paint and decoupage papers. Decoupage is a simple technique—you cut out the desired images and adhere them to a surface—but skill is required for even, accurate cutting. Use a small pair of sharp scissors to cut out decoupage motifs; hold the scissors at an angle close to the edge of the motif as you cut; turn the paper as you cut so that you get a clean edge. If desired, use a crafts knife and a self-healing cutting mat.

Look for decoupage papers in crafts and art supply stores as well as on the Internet. If you can't find special decoupage papers in motifs you like, use wrapping paper or wallpaper, but don't use magazines: The images on the reverse side of the paper will bleed through when you apply the decoupage medium.

You Will Need

Chest or other piece of furniture
Screwdriver
Sandpaper, tack cloth
Paintbrush
Primer
Latex enamel paint in the desired color and finish

Small, sharp scissors
Decoupage papers, wrapping papers, or other desired paper
Decoupage medium, paintbrush or foam brush, sponge, wallpaper smoother

1 Remove any drawers, doors, and hardware from the piece of furniture. Lightly sand each portion; remove any dust with the tack cloth.

2 Prime the piece of furniture; let dry. Paint; let dry.

3 Cut the desired motifs from the paper. Using a paintbrush or foam brush, apply decoupage medium to the back of each motif and adhere to the piece of furniture. If excess decoupage medium seeps from beneath the motifs, quickly wipe it away with a damp sponge.

4 After all motifs are placed, cover the entire surface with a thin, even layer of decoupage medium, using a foam brush to seal. Use the wallpaper smoother to flatten the edges of the papers; this ensures they will adhere to the surface.

5 Reattach the hardware or doors and reinsert the drawers.

❋ For more fresh furniture ideas, visit
HGTV.com/beforeandafterbook

MORE IDEAS FOR

Softening a
Sterile Space

White bathrooms offer a clean, crisp, fresh look, but a lack of color can make a monochromatic room feel devoid of personality. The good news is nearly any color, from primaries to pastels, can work well with white. If your walls are white and you don't want to paint them, bring in color by way of fabrics, for instance, shower curtains, rugs, towels, and accessories.

Wainscoting and board-and-batten molding in crisp white are paired with a white honeycomb tile floor, a vintage bathtub, a terry cloth-covered bench, and sheer curtains in this sunny, style-savvy bath. Walls painted in pale blue set off the white moldings and fixtures.

White fixtures and a black and white tile floor are classics—as are the etched frameless mirror and delicate glass shelf. Hints of pale lilac—paint on the walls, an upholstered stool, and items placed on the sink and glass shelf—breath life into this small powder room.

This attic bath, with its sloping ceilings and limited standing room, is filled with casual charm, from the white beaded board to the lively mix of black and white checked, floral, and dotted patterns. Because moving or replacing a bathtub is messy and costly, painting it is a great option. To paint the outside of a tub similar to this, clean the sides with a trisodium phosphate cleaner, apply a coat of high-quality latex primer, and paint the desired motif with latex or acrylic paints. To clean a painted tub, use a damp sponge and avoid abrasive cleaners.

Respecting the ROOTS

This bathroom in a 1950s ranch hadn't been altered much since its creation. It still functioned well enough, but the dated tiles, dark wood vanity, and worn bathtub were in need of attention. Help came in the form of a fresh color scheme, a dresser-turned-vanity, and sleek accessories that respect—and even enhance—the midcentury roots of this home. If your bathroom still functions well enough but has a dated look, take cues from this stylish transformation.

Start with a clean slate. The first step in this makeover was reevaluating the walls. The paneled walls had been painted white in an earlier redecorating, but rather than try to salvage or recover them, fresh drywall is installed. This provides a clean, even starting point. The fresh turquoise blue paint that now covers the walls is a nod to the '50s; olive green accents throughout the room are the perfect period partner.

Update a tub with paint and graphic elements. To keep the project under budget, the tub is retained, but it required a deep cleaning and repainting with do-it-yourself epoxy paint formulated for the job. To further freshen the tub area, 12x12-inch tile replaces the small yellow tiles, and stainless-steel fixtures are now in place. Finally, ½-inch glass shower screen is mounted to the tub and wall, extending to the ceiling beam for support. The glass is sandblasted in a graphic circular pattern within 12-inch squares.

Restyle furniture for new function. The dark, dual-sink vanity was in good condition, but its boxy shape lacked pizzazz. The rest of the home is filled with midcentury furnishings and accessories, so a vintage dresser found at a secondhand shop seemed a perfect remedy: Fitted with a stainless-steel sink and faucet, the dresser now serves as a hip vanity—and fitting focal point. Above, a green-frame mirror replaces the old plain one, and retro lamps replace uninspired lighting choices. Track lighting is installed on the ceiling beam for good measure.

Continued on page 158

BEFORE

AFTER

Look for storage in unlikely places. The new vanity provides some storage, but not enough. Ready-made cabinet boxes with doors offer a solution. Typically, such boxes are stacked, but here they are staggered on the wall opposite the vanity, where framed photographs once hung. Inside, toiletries and hand towels are stored; black and white photographs grace the exterior doors. The staggered placement allows the tops to be used for displaying period collectibles.

Continue the sleek style throughout the space. To complete the makeover, the vinyl flooring gave way to large ceramic tiles, which link the space with the connecting hallway tiles. The old inefficient toilet is replaced with a contemporary one-piece unit that complements the sleek styling throughout the room.

BEFORE

AFTER

Dresser Vanity

Transforming a dresser into a vanity is a fun way to make your bathroom one of a kind. First, choose a dresser that's in good condition and in dimensions that suit your space; check that it will accommodate the size and style of sink you desire. If you are skilled at plumbing, you can hook up the plumbing yourself; otherwise, hire a professional plumber to do the work for you.

You Will Need
Dresser
Sink, faucet
Optional: pencil, scissors, paper
Marker, masking tape
Jigsaw
Screwdriver

1. Decide where you want the sink to be placed on the dresser top. Remove the drawers and any drawer supports that will interfere with the plumbing.

2. Most sinks come with a positioning template; if yours does not, trace the sink outline and create one with paper. Tape the template in the desired place on the dresser top; trace. If you will be mounting the faucet outside the sink, as in this example, mark its placement too.

3. Determine the location of the water supply and drain lines. Mark this location on the back of the dresser.

4. Using a jigsaw, cut the sink, faucet, and water supply/drain line openings.

5. Set the sink and faucet, following the manufacturer's instructions. Hook up the plumbing.

6. Cut the backs of the drawers that surround the sink and/or plumbing so that they fit perfectly into place. Use the jigsaw to remove the necessary portions.

7. Reinsert the drawers.

MORE IDEAS FOR

Storage

Any bathroom—large or small, new or old—can benefit from increased storage capacity. Whether you need a place to keep grooming and cleaning supplies, or a place for towels and linens, or both, finding attractive, space-savvy options can be problematic. Many of the ideas shown can be incorporated into a new or remodeled bath. Also, put to use overlooked spaces such as your walls and the back of a door; hooks, racks, and pegs can hold towels and robes.

These may look like swing-out doors, but they actually glide like drawers so that nothing becomes hidden in the back. Even the space around the plumbing is put to good use, thanks to a ring that holds a hand towel.

Decorative panels on the front of a vanity can also serve a purpose: Use them for handy tilt-out storage. Kits available at home improvement centers often include hinges and a shelf that attaches to the back of the panel. The panel shown here hides an electrical outlet.

If your medicine chest is an eyesore, replace the door with a cut-to-fit wooden panel inside a wooden frame and apply a print for instant appeal. Nonglare glass protects the paper from moisture.

The space between bathroom wall studs is an ideal place for a tall, narrow storage niche. This in-shower space has plenty of room for towels; a small glass shelf keeps bath oils and other accessories within reach.

A sliding drawer pulls out easily, and everything stored within is in plain view. Dividers keep the items organized. Tall bottles are placed on the side; small items stay in the shallow middle section beneath the plumbing.

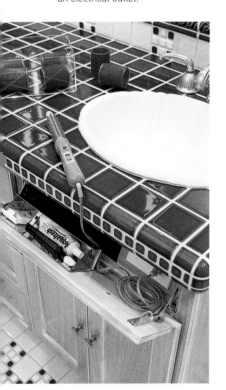

Warming Up a
MASTER BATH

Left with typical builder finishes after construction, a master bath like this one has all the warmth and charm of a high school locker room. All it takes, however, is a little vision and a pinch of cash to turn lackluster into luxurious.

Play up what you have. If your bath looks similar to this, create a plan that allows you to keep the existing fixtures and cabinetry, for cost-effectiveness. The cabinets in this bath were plain white, but rich brown paint really warms up the room; the gold-tone faucets already on the tub and sink added a nice glamorous touch, so they are kept; the cabinet hardware is replaced with brass-tone traditional pieces that match the new style of the room. The green marble-look flooring was not worn, so the smart choice was to keep the flooring and develop a color scheme that would complement—rather than match—the dark green.

Color and pattern add interest. A chocolate-brown on cream toile wallpaper is the perfect backdrop for the relaxed, high-country look. The scenic toile pattern flows in an easy manner across the large expanse of wall. Two plush rugs in a cream color break up the field of marble and brighten the floor.

Continued on page 164

STYLISH FURNISHINGS

Once you've made the color and style choices for a room, start planning complementary touches, items that give a room—even a bath—its style. These details make the difference between a functional and uninviting bathroom and a relaxing, spa-like space. Go beyond the obvious towels, rugs, and soap holders and add the elements you'd find in any comfortable room:

- **Upholstered chair.** Include a small, comfortable chair to sit on after a bath or when getting dressed. An armless parsons chair, like the one in this room, is small and light enough to be easily moved around the bath as needed.
- **Cushioned bench.** A bench provides a nice focal point on a long, blank wall. The open legs on the bench shown here keep the look light. The cushioned seat is the perfect place to lay a robe or slippers. Cover the cushion with fabric that matches or complements other fabric used in the room.
- **Wall art.** High-quality artwork in interesting frames makes any bathroom seem more luxurious. When choosing artwork, choose pieces that will resist temperature and humidity. Mirrors with interesting frames, unusual shapes, or decorative etching are both functional and artistic additions to a bathroom.
- **Accessories.** In any room little things make the difference, so include an artful mix of small ceramic, glass, or porcelain pieces in your bath. For a garden touch, use these pieces to hold fresh flowers or small plants.
- **Plant stand.** In a bathroom with a large soaking tub like this one, include a tubside table to keep a cup of tea, a book, or a loofah at hand. It's perfect for keeping items away from the edge of the tub but at your fingertips.

BEFORE

AFTER

AFTER

BEFORE

Layered window treatments offer versatility. A pair of windows placed side by side create the effect of one large window over the tub. This arrangement lets in lots of light, but it needed the right window treatment to provide privacy. A brown-check custom-made valance hung well over the top of the window frame—only 2 inches from the ceiling—makes the window unit look even larger. Behind the valance is a custom Roman shade in an off-white diamond matelassé with a brown-check banding to provide the required privacy.

Bathrooms need display space too. A narrow shelf runs the width of both windows. Painted a glossy white and held in place with decorative brackets, the shelf extends the lower frame of the window and is the perfect place for a few plants to accent the green tile.

SMART MONEY

Window treatments can be budget-busters, but in a room where the window is a key feature, custom window treatments can be worth the investment. This Roman shade, made of a good fabric with custom trim and a perfectly pleated valance, would be a hard project for anyone who hasn't done it before. Because this window is a relatively modest size, the cost of the custom work wasn't overwhelming.

Display Shelf

Simple shelves below or above a window make a stylish statement, whether they display keepsakes or everyday items. Your local home improvement center has everything you need, including MDF (medium-density fiberboard) to make a shelf such as this. Choose a bracket style and size that complements the look of the room and has the right depth for the shelf.

You Will Need

Tape measure
Saw
MDF (see Step 1 for size)
Primer, latex paint in the desired
   color and finish, paintbrush

2 decorative brackets with hardware
Stud finder
Screwdriver

1 ▪ Measure the window width. Cut the MDF to this length and 6 to 8 inches wide.

2 ▪ Prime the shelf and brackets; let dry. Paint; let dry.

3 ▪ Install the brackets on the wall studs so they align with the edges of the frame; this makes the shelf look as though it is part of the window.

4 ▪ Top the brackets with the shelf.

FAUX-CHERRY CABINETS

The cabinets in this bath received a rich cherry-look paint treatment. For a similar effect, after priming, apply a light brown paint; let dry. Apply a dark brown glaze to the surface, working in 1-foot-square sections. Immediately wipe off excess glaze using a dry cotton rag to achieve a mottled effect. Continue the process until all surfaces are covered and ragged; let dry. Apply a brown-red glaze with a 2-inch-wide paintbrush, working in a 1-foot-square area. While the glaze is still wet, drag a wood-graining tool over the area, revealing some of the base coat paint and mottled glaze. Continue the process until the entire piece is covered. Seal with a coat of polyurethane.

✳ For more do-it-yourself shelf projects, visit **HGTV.com/beforeandafterbook**

MORE OR

Fabric Touches

Like any other room of the house, bathrooms can benefit from doses of fabric color and pattern. Whether your bath is large or small or has charming vintage fixtures or brand-new features, it can be softened or given a high-energy spark with shower curtains, sink and toilet skirts, window treatments, and even upholstered chairs and footstools. If you have fabric scraps left from a project, use them to cover a photo frame, embellish a ready-made towel, or line a basket that holds toiletries.

Hand-painted stripes on the walls, along with cottage-style fabrics in various prints and patterned picture frames, give this basic bath a colorful spark. The sink skirt conceals unsightly pipes, while the minimal window treatments let in maximum sunlight.

A mix of fabrics, including terry cloth, a sheer stripe, and a black and beige check, bring pattern into this bath. The floor-length curtain is tucked behind the ceiling soffit; fringed trim edges the soffit and is attached to the shower side of the overhang with hook-and-loop tape. A fabric valance hides a 1x1 that has a sheer striped fabric stapled to it. To embellish ordinary hand towels, use snaps or hook-and-loop tape to attach pompom trim and rickrack, which can be removed for washing.

Vintage floral fabrics impart a cottage-style look to this bath. Bedsheets are fashioned into a shower curtain; the window treatment is a restyled curtain panel. The corners of the panel are nailed into the beaded board, and the nailheads are hidden by large glued-on buttons. Strips of fabric accent the treatment and give it shape. Another piece of fabric is attached to the underside of the vanity with hook-and-loop tape to conceal the sink pipes.

A remnant of white and green plaid fabric acts as a simple window shade that lets in sunlight. A tighter green plaid serves as a shower curtain. The bright green fabrics, along with a hand-painted green and blue wave border, enliven the space.

CHOOSING BATHROOM FABRICS

When selecting fabrics for your bathroom, keep these tips in mind:

- **Who will use it—and how often.** If the bathroom is used infrequently—and by adults only—luxurious fabrics that will receive little handling work fine. If the bathroom is strictly for children, purchase practical laminated shower curtains that can stand up to wear and tear.
- **Choose washable, natural fabrics that are easy to care for, including cotton, cotton blend, or linen.** Wash them in cold water, dry on low heat, and smooth out wrinkles with a cool iron.
- **Avoid using stain-prone fabrics or ones that have to be dry-cleaned.** Silk will show water stains, and heavy upholstery fabric often requires dry cleaning.

Country Checks to
CLEAN AND SERENE

Boxy rooms with no architectural detail are easy spaces to wallpaper, but they may lack character. This bathroom suffered from exactly that, with a dated checked wallcovering, a generic vanity, plain plate glass mirror, and exposed-bulb lighting. Help came in the form of beaded-board wainscoting, a light-color patterned wallcovering, and molding details that transform the space from dowdy to dramatic.

Beaded board adds charm. Sixty-inch-tall beaded-board paneling covers the lower portion of the walls. The white-painted paneling is only ¼ inch thick, which works especially well for small rooms that can't afford to lose square footage to the walls. To install, the tiled baseboard was removed, and the paneling was glued and nailed to the drywall. The decorative molding cap adds much-needed detailing. Beaded board also makes an appearance on the vanity doors.

Use color to provide a sense of spaciousness. To visually expand the small space, a light-color wallpaper with a swirling scroll motif covers the upper portion of the walls and flows onto the ceiling for a seamless transition. The white-painted vanity and mirror frame keep the room light and airy. The new white countertop—actually 12-inch marble tiles adhered to the existing countertop—freshens the surface for little cost. The tiles are attached with thin set, and latex grout fills in the gaps between tiles. A 1½-inch wood trim covers the tile and old laminate edge.
Continued on page 170

BEFORE

AFTER

Give the mirror focal-point status. The most dramatic change in this space is the made-over mirror. The homemade frame fills the space between the vanity and ceiling and gives the once plain mirror a grand appearance. A new light fixture is attached directly to the mirror for effective general lighting.

Pay attention to details. Completing the look, new towel bars have the same finish and style as the light fixture and brushed-nickel cabinetry hardware. The vanity basket contains soaps and other small items previously jumbled on the vanity corner. Framed artwork fills the space between the door frame and mirror, taking the place of two small wreaths that were out of proportion in the room.

PAINTING CABINETS AND OTHER WOOD FURNISHINGS

The misconception that all wood is good wood needs to be let go. Good wood tones do warm a room, but many wood surfaces are not meant to be exposed and are best painted over. The cabinets in this bathroom are a case in point.

Painting over lesser-grade woods isn't difficult, but it does require some care to get a good finish. First, wash the surface with a good-quality wood cleaner. Anything that's been in the air could be on the furniture surface.

Remove all hardware; if you're changing it, use wood putty to close the holes. Completely fill the holes and sand the surface completely smooth. Give the entire surface a good sanding to add some tooth for the best paint adhesion. Wipe down the entire piece with a tack cloth to remove all dust particles. A smooth surface is crucial for a good painted finish. Wood grain can be rather forgiving; some minor nicks and dings aren't noticeable. Furniture painted a solid color will show every nuance in the surface.

A satin-finish paint will give a final surface that's luxurious but not slick or glossy-looking. It will also be easy to take care of. Most pieces require two coats or more, and to ensure the best finish, allow adequate drying time between coats and sand between coats.

On heavily used surfaces, such as the top of a dresser or cabinet doors that may require scrubbing, adding a couple of coats of water-base polyurethane will help seal the surface and protect it from everyday scratches, nicks, and water rings.

Framed Mirror

One of the easiest ways to give a mirror importance is with molding. This framing project will dress up any bath. In the example shown, a light fixture is mounted directly onto the mirror. If you choose to do this, you will need to cut a hole in the mirror over the light box.

You Will Need
Tape measure
Saw
1x6 boards (4)
Hammer, nails
1x4 boards (2)
Sandpaper, tack cloth

Primer, paint in the desired color
   and finish, paintbrush
1x2 trim
Mirror
5" crown molding
Glue
Mirror mounting hardware
Stud finder

1 ▣ Measure the mirror. Cut the 1x6 board into four pieces to frame the mirror; nail together.

2 ▣ Rip the 1x4 boards to 3 inches wide; cut to fit around the frame. Nail in place.

3 ▣ Sand the frame; remove any dust with the tack cloth. Prime; let dry. Paint; let dry. Also sand, prime, and paint the 1x2 trim and crown molding.

4 ▣ Glue the mirror into the frame; let dry. Cut the 1x2 trim to serve as the innermost frame that will keep the mirror secure. Nail in place.

5 ▣ Top the frame with the crown molding; nail in place.

6 ▣ Mount the framed mirror to the wall, attaching it to the wall studs.

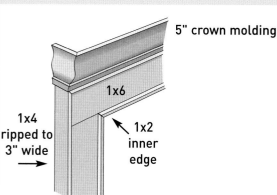

5" crown molding

1x6

1x4
ripped to
3" wide

1x2
inner
edge

MORE IDEAS FOR

Mirrors and Lights

Because bathrooms are the designated place for grooming, mirrors and lights are essential to their function. To ensure your bathroom mirror is evenly illuminated and free of shadows, light sources need to be evenly distributed around it. If movie star lights—exposed bulbs that surround the entire mirror—don't appeal to you, plan to install one or two fixtures above the mirror that cast light over the front edge of the sink and countertop; two additional lights—one centered on each side of the mirror—will ensure even lighting. If there isn't enough room for lights on the sides of your mirror, consider a light above the mirror that is longer than the mirror itself. When paired with a light-color countertop, more light will reflect on your face. When purchasing bulbs for your bathroom, select those designed for vanity illumination, which create light in the daylight spectrum range; bulbs that are too yellow or white will not create an accurate reflection of how you look outside the bathroom. For more information on lightbulb selection and the three types of lighting—general, task, and accent—see pages 52 and 53.

◀ Matching the width of each vanity, the framed mirrors feature tubes of incandescent lighting that emphasize the other strong vertical lines in the room.

▶ Wall sconces and light fixtures recessed in an overhang illuminate tall mirrors set into the maple-clad wall in this bathroom.

▼ Rectangular mirrors above both vanities play up the rectangular sinks and rows of small windows (reflected in the mirror), unifying the space. Thanks to the multiple windows, natural light fills this room so the sconces beside the mirrors provide adequate light.

▲ A thrift store mirror makes a bold statement in this dramatic bath. It hangs from the ceiling on a piece of black and gold rope. Recessed lights above the vanity supplement natural light from a large window behind the vanity.

◀ The mirrors in this bathroom have curved tops, which repeat the curves of the vanity below. Light fixtures installed on the sides of each mirror pair with recessed fixtures above for even illumination. The white walls help reflect light.

MIRROR HEIGHT

To ensure that people of different heights can comfortably use a mirror, it is generally recommended that the bottom edge of a mirror be hung no more than 40 inches from the floor. If the top of the mirror is tilted away from the wall, its bottom edge can be as much as 48 inches above the floor.

Options, Options, OPTIONS

Sometimes a bathroom has everything going for it—great flooring, plenty of natural light, a roomy tub—but without creative accessorizing, even the most stylish elements don't live up to their potential. Two different looks, bold contemporary and French country, are created in this bath, using three basic elements: functional bathroom items, such as towels, candles, and soaps; simple window treatments; and wall art, rugs, and natural elements for warmth and texture.

OPTION ONE: CONTEMPORARY

The black and white floor tiles lend themselves to this punchy color scheme of chartreuse and salmon and interesting graphic elements.

Make a bold, graphic statement. Squares appear throughout the space, from the houndstooth check of the window valance to the square artwork that flanks the tub. The bright fruit paintings, typically reserved for kitchens and dining areas, bring a playful element into the bath. Another piece of art, an abstract painting, is propped against the wall on the tub ledge.

Don't forget the fun. The flowers and greenery, including a flat of grass on the tub ledge and gerbera daisies on the vanity, keep the look fresh and springlike. The vase with green and bronze-color dots adds a contemporary note; so do the black accents, including a mesh storage basket that holds towels at the base of the tub.

Repeat the colors for emphasis. Chartreuse and salmon accents abound in towels, candles, and other inexpensive vanity accessories. The bright green also makes an appearance on the bench cushion and funky floral-motif rug.

Continued on page 176

BEFORE

OPTION ONE: CONTEMPORARY

Although black and white looks perfect in a contemporary scheme, it can easily suit a more refined look when paired with muted colors—in this case, soft peach-pink and celadon green—and thoughtfully placed accessories.

Fabric changes the look. The window treatments are of the same design as the ones in the contemporary bath, but the black and white toile fabric gives them a completely different, more tailored, look. This same toile now graces the bench cushion.

Refine with texture. Wicker and copper are the dominant textural elements in this refined bath. From the French wall basket filled with greenery and the basket urn on the tub ledge to the various copper pots throughout the room, a high-country look prevails. A toile-lined basket provides stylish storage for towels and slippers, and a basket tray artfully contains vanity clutter.

ARTFULLY CONTAINED

To reduce clutter in the bath—and bring in interesting shapes, colors, and textures—group lotions, soaps, and other necessities on pretty trays and platters or in baskets and bowls. In the French take on this bath a white-painted urn stores cotton swabs on the sink vanity tray, and a glass jar filled with soaps echoes the smooth lines of the tub. In the bold, contemporary version a bright green plate holds colorful bathroom accessories on the vanity.

OPTION TWO: FRENCH COUNTRY

MORE IDEAS FOR

Accessorizing the Bath

Envision a relaxing sanctuary; then picture it in your own bathroom. Start with a mental image or a real image, such as a picture, postcard, or another source of inspiration. After you envision the perfect scene, select a color palette. Determine which colors evoke the setting you want to capture; pick one or two dominant colors as well as a complementary accent or neutral tone. Next, what textures work in your theme? Can they be incorporated in flooring or window treatments? Finally, to pull your theme into focus, add decorative accents, including pictures, keepsakes, artwork, or plants.

Seemingly diverse elements—antique Dutch tiles, chartreuse paint, and beaded-board wainscoting—come together and dress up a once dingy, dark bath. The colorful wall art is the perfect accompaniment to the deep molding display shelf, which holds a collection of pottery from the '40s and '50s. The sink features chrome pipe fittings and a marble top.

This tiny bath gets a boost in style from wallpaper that features large architectural elements such as columns and busts. Books on built-in shelves, an antique dresser, and framed prints in black and white create a library look.

Vintage photographs and antique accessories—along with a claw-foot tub, oak plank floors, and tongue-and-groove siding used as wainscoting—transport this bath to the country. All the wood surfaces have been antiqued to impart the feeling of an old rural dwelling.

Can there be too much of a good theme? The answer is no in this delightful dog-theme bath. Dogs march across the walls, and paw prints embellish the sink and medicine cabinet. Neutral striped fabrics appear as a sink skirt and a clever window valance that includes dog biscuits attached with twine.

SPECIAL SPACES

Refining a
FOCAL POINT

With only minor changes, yesterday's dark and dated fireplace can become a bright and fresh focal point. The fireplace here had ample display and storage space in the form of bookcases, but the dark wood and brick and cluttered shelves created an eyesore rather than a pleasing visual bonus. In addition, dark beams, which served only a decorative purpose, made the room feel small and cavernlike. A new color palette and enhanced architectural details—with some contemporary elements thrown in for interest—give the room sophisticated flair.

Remove the old. First, the ceiling beams were removed. Fortunately, only minor patching was required where the beams were attached. The heavy brown crown molding also was removed; white crown molding now frames the entire room. A fresh coat of white paint covers the ceiling and a light marble-pattern wallpaper (applied in pieces to look like a painted faux finish) makes the room look larger and more open.

Update and unify with paint and moldings. The elements in the wall unit lacked unity: A mantel shelf was hung with little consideration for the style of the hearth or fireplace surround. A new mantel, made of crown molding and fluted pilasters, now surrounds the fireplace to make it the center of the focal point. The brickwork and the bookcase are painted white. To further emphasize the center, the bricks are treated to a subtle beige colorwashing, and a crackle-finish screen rests on the hearth.

Continued on page 184

BEFORE

AFTER

Create visual impact. Before painting, the bookcases received their own special treatment: Extra moldings add heft to balance the heavy visual weight of the brick. Doors are added to the lower portions of the cases for closed storage; the vertical lines of the doors break up the strong horizontal lines created by the stacked shelves. Built-in benches provide extra seating and ground the focal point wall. Gentle arches make an appearance in the curved top of the bookcases, doors, and bench fronts. The curves soften distinct lines present throughout the space and create a cohesive look; if one curve motif alone were introduced, it would look out of place, but repeating the motif enhances its impact.

Visually soften the hearth. To complete the focal-point makeover, tile replaces the brick on the hearth. Framed in wood, the tile has a softer visual appearance than the brick, and it is much easier to clean.

Complete the look with color—and comfort. New wood laminate flooring, which replaced worn gray carpeting, warms up the floor and updates the overall look. The black-trim rug defines the space. To add further character, wood-tone accessories, both old and new, soften the dominant white and make it appear less formal. The chair is re-covered in soft, supple imitation suede, which takes it from dowdy to dramatic; with a side table and reading lamp, it's now a great place to relax and read a book. For a contemporary kick, curved track lighting and door hardware in brushed nickel add a touch of modern simplicity.

▶ Cabinet doors and a pair of benches provide hidden storage. A gentle curve motif on the door and bench fronts mimics the arch on the top of the bookcases.

▶ Updating a tired but stylish chair is as easy as reupholstering it. In this case, faux suede in a soft brown covers the chair cushions, complementing the warm tones in the room. Details include black circles, cut from more faux suede, and nailhead tacks, both of which repeat the cutwork detailing on the original chair.

◀ Crown molding frames the room and poses as the new mantel shelf. Repetition and reuse of key elements strengthens any design scheme.

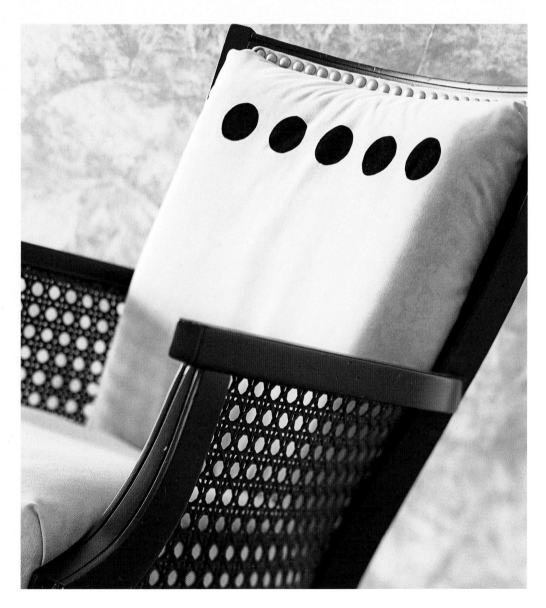

MORE IDEAS FOR
Fireplace Mantels

Fireplaces usually take center stage in a room—but is your focal point lacking pizzazz? Whether your mantel is new or old, brick or wood, it can benefit from a makeover. Use these examples as a springboard to create a space that commands attention.

Paint is one of the easiest ways to freshen a mantel. Once a generic builder mantel, this example now sports a neutral beige paint with red details that complement the surrounding wall. The recessed areas are painted with a contemporary-look marble finish.

Layered tiles in woodsy colors and motifs form a fresh facade over a dingy, outdated brick fireplace. Because ripping out the brick would have been labor-intensive, a layer of cement mortar was troweled on and allowed to cure for a week to provide a smooth, solid surface. The tiles are applied with thin-set tile adhesive; terra-cotta-color sanded grout fills in the seams.

Columns and a mercury-glass mirror frame an old wood fireplace surround that has a well-worn painted finish. These details bring a sense of history and architectural significance to the living room. The surround replaced faux stones.

A flat brick-face fireplace is given the royal treatment with a wood cover-up. The basic structure is covered with a combination of stock moldings—including fluted pilasters, dentil trim, and a deep crown—and painted with a fresh coat of semi-gloss white to brighten the room and lend simple elegance.

Underutilized to STYLIZED

A clean, uncluttered entryway may appear open and bright, but it isn't necessarily functional. Rather than leave this space unused, make it say "Wow!" In this new home, the entryway was bare, with little more than a table in place. A clean, modern look steps in, courtesy of thoughtfully placed storage and seating pieces and a new paint treatment. If you are faced with a similar situation, take advantage of the underused area. How would you like it to function? Do you need a place to change footwear or primp before heading to work or an evening on the town? Can you take advantage of storage possibilities? Here, all these issues are addressed.

Readymade seating and storage increase functionality. First, a set of ready-made cubes—some open and others with drawers and doors—is arranged in a step system that draws the eye to the window, the only existing architectural element in the space. The cubes are used for display, and the low, comfy seating area is a great place to sort mail. This unit effectively fills the space between the coat closet to the left and the pillar that divides the entry from the main living space.

Define the space with color. The ceiling in this space is high. To bring the walls down to scale—and to keep the eye interested in what's happening down low—the wall behind the unit is painted in two colors. Using the top of the pillar as a natural breaking point, soft blue-green is painted below, and white is painted above, framing the space for an intimate setting. Where the two colors meet, dentil molding is painted metallic silver. Squares stenciled in silver leaf, spaced randomly on the walls, complement the metallic look. The square motif imitates the cube design and provides a shiny accent on the walls.

Continued on page 190

BEFORE

AFTER

Mirror magic. A mirror is always a welcome addition to an entryway. Here, a custom-cut oval mirror fills the space between the window and the higher cubes. Mounted on pivot brackets, it can accommodate users of any height. The nearby lamp provides functional and task lighting for mirror use and accent lighting for the display.

Accessorize with contrasting color and shapes. Modern clean-line accessories in a variety of shapes introduce color and contrast against the predominantly green and black space. Silver makes an appearance in photo frames and the lamp base, complementing the cube hardware and legs. A piece of pottery, painted in two colors, and the striped rug continue the strong graphic lines that define the space.

STENCILED IN SILVER

Metallic silver leaf in a random square design brings subtle color into this space. For a similar look, purchase a square stencil, or create one yourself with a piece of clear acetate and a crafts knife. Using stencil adhesive, adhere the stencil to the wall in the desired location. Following the manufacturer's instructions, carefully apply the leaf to the wall (the material is delicate and tears easily). Move the stencil to the next desired location and apply the leaf in the stencil opening.

Hinged Mirror

Mirrors play a necessary role in entryways, but ensuring that a guest or resident of any height can use the mirror is an important consideration. This mirror is set on pivoting hinges so it can be angled upward or downward to accommodate all who use it. Evaluate the space you need to fill. Mirrors are available in many shapes and sizes, but you may need to have one cut to best fit your needs. Be aware that brackets will not hold a beveled-edge mirror.

You Will Need

Tape measure
Scissors
Adhesive-back foam
2 pivoting brackets and hardware

Mirror
Screwdriver
Stud finder

1. Measure the mirror and determine the best placement of the side brackets; center the brackets on the sides to ensure the mirror will hang straight.

2. Cut four pieces of adhesive-back foam the same size as the portion of the bracket that will hold the mirror in place. Peel off the backing and press the foam onto the mirror in the location determined in Step 1.

3. Using the screwdriver, tighten the brackets to secure the mirror.

4. Mount the mirror to the wall, directly to the wall studs.

3

✳ For hundreds of ideas on using mirrors effectively in your home, visit **HGTV.com/beforeandafterbook**

MORE IDEAS FOR

Functional Entryways

Entryways offer guests the first glimpse into your home and its style. Encourage guests to linger—and make a strong first impression—by filling the space with personal touches, such as collections, or by placing comfortable furnishings nearby for removing footwear. Include a rack or pegs for hanging jackets and hats and a mirror that will both visually enlarge the space and provide a practical place to groom before leaving the house.

White wainscoting beneath soft blue walls sheathes this entryway, a former bedroom. Hooks provide spots to hang jackets and hats, and an antique table is the perfect spot to drop mail and keys.

Greeting guests with things you love gives them a taste for what's beyond the entryway. In this space a 300-year-old table, black tole tray, and flow-blue pieces introduce guests to a home filled with history.

This entryway, with its vivid painted walls, moon-motif clock, and playful bench, prepares visitors for more visual excitement inside. The tile floor is easy to clean, and the mirror permits last-minute primping before departure.

This entry/mudroom features nautical references: Color copies of French nautical charts are pasted above the tall wainscoting; the round mirrors are reminiscent of portholes. Hooks accept jackets and beach bags, and a large basket on the floor can hold umbrellas and other outdoor necessities.

Carving Out a Corner for COMFORT

Small homes often have less than abundant storage space. This 900-square foot home is a case in point. Although the home-owners haven't amassed a huge number of possessions, they still require a place to store blankets, pillows, books, and keepsakes in their bedroom. Rather than purchase or create freestanding storage units that might take up too much precious space, they found an ingenious solution: a window seat with storage beneath (the lid lifts for easy access to items). The cozy space is perfect for catching a nap or reading beneath the window.

The look of a bump-out—without remodeling. This window seat, which is nearly the dimensions of a twin-size bed, was constructed against a flat interior bedroom wall. Typically, window seats are added via a bump-out, but the architecture of the home and an old tree right outside the window ruled out that option. A vertical box forms a closet to the left of the window seat, and the window seat itself is a horizontal box, which fills in the space between the closet and the wall to create the feel of a bump-out.

Luxurious fabrics add color and comfort. Upholstered medium-density foam tops the bench, making it a haven for the homeowners—or young overnight visitors who can use it as a bed. Pillows of varying sizes invite people to come and stay for a while. The pillows are made of silks in a mix of warm and cool colors that spice up the overall neutral color palette. Light affects how the silks appear: During the day they are a bold counterpoint to the beige walls, but in the evening the colors deepen for a more romantic appearance.

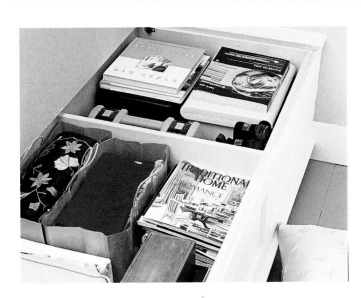

The lid of this window seat lifts to reveal storage space. The seat holds seasonal bedding, books, and magazines. The contents are kept organized thanks to dividers.

BEFORE

AFTER

Obi Pillow

Pillows can serve as jewelry for your room—and this dynamic design with an obi (which resembles the sash traditionally worn with a kimono) is no exception. Splurging on luxurious fabrics gives this pillow a special feel and look. Anyone with basic sewing skills can stitch pillows. If you choose to use silk brocade and douppioni silk, as shown here, you will need to use special care: These fabrics unravel quickly, so carefully cut on the straight of grain with clean, sharp scissors or a rotary cutter. Serge the edges or use a specially formulated ravel preventer. Otherwise, use an easier-to-handle fabric such as cotton.

You Will Need

Scissors or rotary cutter
13x12" pieces of silk brocade for
    pillow back (2)
13x17" piece of silk brocade for
    pillow front
Sewing machine, matching thread,
    70/10H needle, presser foot

Pins
Iron, ironing board
Chopstick
Satin cording
Ravel preventer
4x26" pieces of douppioni silk (2)
12x16" pillow form
Tailor's chalk

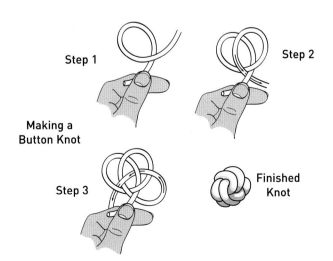

Step 1

Step 2

Making a Button Knot

Step 3

Finished Knot

1. Create a double-fold machine hem on the inside edge of each pillow back piece. Place the back flaps on the pillow front with right sides facing, overlapping the hemmed edges of the back pieces. Carefully pin the pieces together and stitch around the perimeter, using a ½-inch seam allowance. To avoid pointy dog-ear corners, taper the seam at each corner.

2. Turn the pillow cover right side out, using the chopstick to gently push out the corners; press.

3. To create the button knots for the obi sash, you will need 8 to 10 inches of satin cording. Loop the cord as shown in the illustrations, then ease the knot together into a ball shape and finish with a simple knot. Squeeze and pinch to define the ball shape. Repeat the process to make a second knot. Trim the ends of each knot and treat with ravel preventer.

4. To make the button loops, use 3 inches of satin cording and shape into a teardrop large enough to accommodate the button, leaving ½-inch-long tails; baste. Repeat the process to make a second loop.

5. To make the obi, use the 4x26-inch pieces of douppioni silk. Pin the two pieces together with right sides facing and stitch around the perimeter, using a ½-inch seam allowance and leaving one end open. Turn the obi right side out and gently push out the corners with the chopstick. Fold in the open end of one piece of silk approximately ½ inch. Baste the loops made in Step 4 to the folded-in piece of silk, 1⅛ inches from each side. Fold in the other piece of silk approximately ½ inch and slip-stitch closed. Fit the sash around the pillow, overlapping the ends with the loops on the top. Using the loops as a guide, carefully mark the spot for each button on the obi with tailor's chalk. Blindstitch each button in place.

Storage Window Seat

This window seat, which is essentially a horizontal box, measures 76 inches long by 28 inches high by 27 inches deep. Your project size will be determined by the space available, any architectural restrictions (for instance, window trim), and the cushion thickness, so measure carefully, taking these items into consideration when planning. Note that kickspace is not figured into these instructions; kickspace will be determined by your baseboard molding.

You Will Need

¾" thick medium-density fiberboard (MDF) (3 sheets)
4 pressed-brass surface-mounted hinges or a piano hinge
2 childproof lid supports
6¾" thick x 3" wide x 8' long stock pine

Yellow construction glue
Screws, nails, brads
Primer, latex paint in the desired color and finish, paintbrush
Drill
Hammer
Screwdriver

CONSTRUCTION NOTES

- Follow the illustration to construct the box with a series of dado joints (joints made with rectangular grooves cut into the wood).
- For added strength—and more-organized storage—divide the box into three sections using dado joints.
- The top of the bench box is trimmed with 3-inch-wide pine to support the lid and finished cabinet. The lid is one large, heavy piece of MDF, but you could divide the lid into smaller, more manageable, sections.
- Use childproof lid supports so the lid won't accidentally slam shut on fingers. Use the appropriate size supports for the weight of the lid.
- For added safety, consider drilling ventilation holes into the box cabinet face, using a decorative pattern, so that a child trapped inside could still breathe.
- The applied panel-style face frame is a series of ½-inch-thick by 3-inch-wide MDF strips spaced to suit, then glued and nailed with brads. This gives the window seat a classic finish detail.
- The window seat pictured here is permanently installed in an older home. To compensate for the uneven floor, a basic kick space base was fabricated on-site; the box was made level front to back and side to side with shims and a 4-foot level. The bench box was then placed on the preinstalled kickspace base (it was screwed down and trimmed out, and the lid was added).
- Although the interior of this seat is left unfinished, you could paint it or line it with cedar veneer.

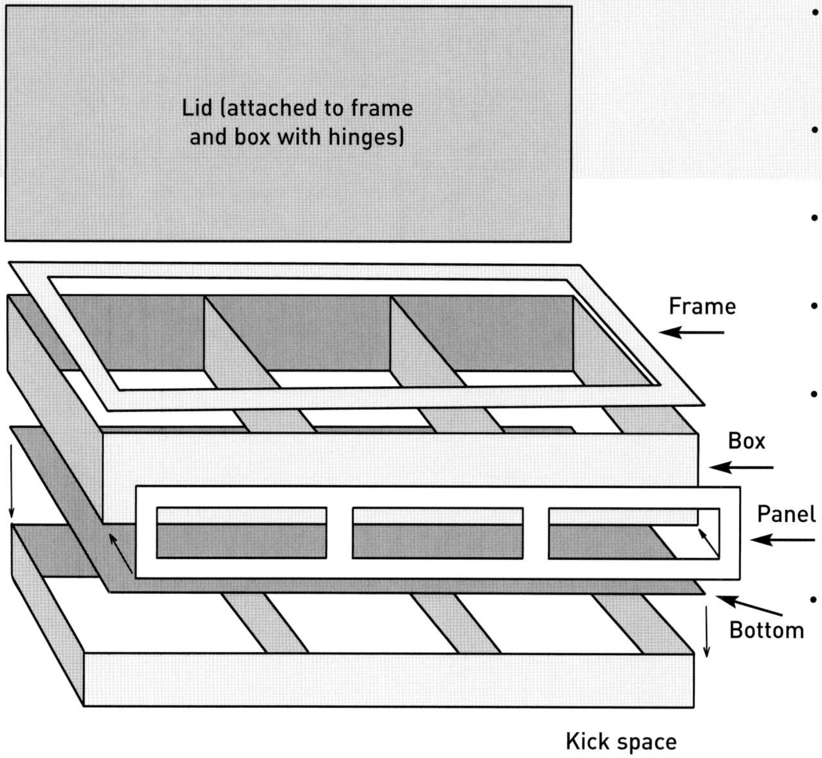

Lid (attached to frame and box with hinges)

Frame

Box

Panel

Bottom

Kick space

MORE IDEAS FOR
Cozy Nooks

Everyone needs a peaceful place to call his or her own—that place where you can hide away for a few moments and read a book, catch a nap, or merely watch the outside world go by. If you don't currently have such a refuge, or the opportunity to create a built-in window seat, take heart: A carefully placed sofa can fulfill your getaway needs.

This entryway niche near the staircase is a convenient place to change footwear. The wood sofa isn't a built-in, but it nestles quite naturally into the spot. A cushion and decorative pillows add comfort.

In this bedroom, a graceful contoured sofa sits between two tall bookcases. It is large enough to accommodate an afternoon napper.

The window seat in this kitchen boasts garden views. It is a wonderful place to chat with the cook while meals are prepared. The drawers beneath hold files.

Nestled between built-in armoires that store clothing and a TV, a gracious window seat is right at home in this bedroom. The seat is a great place to curl up with a book, and the drawers beneath the seat provide additional storage.

Collect It, DISPLAY IT

If you are a collector—or merely have lots of stuff to stash—you undoubtedly have many items to contain and display in one space. If you have a bookcase or open shelving, you may be wondering where to begin. How do you group items? What about incorporating objects of different colors or types? Can you hang art on the walls around the display? In this example, a bookcase is filled with three types of collections; use it as a road map to plot your display strategy.

The bookcase features closed storage below and open shelving above. The shelves can be completely exposed or viewed through glass-fronted doors. The interior of the case has a green distressed paint treatment that provides a subtly aged backdrop against which the items stand out.

VERSION ONE: THE GARDEN THEME

Garden books—vintage and new. Wooden gardening supplies. Brightly colored sap buckets. A small antique landscape painting. Seed packets. An old watering can. If you love gardening and all things natural, you probably have a similar collection gathering dust in your potting shed. Bringing these items together in an artful way transforms them into a unified collection.

Continue a theme throughout a space for added impact. On the wall surrounding the bookcase, tin sap buckets serve as art. These are left empty, but they could easily be filled with flowers, grasses, or even twigs to bring in more of the outside. More buckets—tall, short, cylindrical—stand on top of the cabinet, creating a colorful focal point against the soft beige walls.

To round out the garden theme, floral-motif pillows occupy the chair, and the coffee table houses stacks of garden and landscaping books.

Continued on page 202

Version One: The Garden Theme

Version Two: The White Theme

When arranging a collection in a bookcase or cabinet that has glass-fronted doors, consider how the contents will appear when the doors are closed. Will some items disappear completely behind the door frame? Will some be only partially visible? Plan your design with this in mind, rearranging the items if necessary for viewing.

VERSION TWO: THE WHITE THEME

Mixing old and new items is a breeze when you concentrate on color as a visual link. A mix of objects will make the collection look as if it grew over time; having too many similar items can make your display look like a gift shop shelf. In a group the white ironstone and stoneware platters, pitchers, cake plates, and bowls placed in and on this bookcase (shown on page 201) take on importance—much more than if the pieces were spread throughout the house. Against the green-painted cabinet interior, the white visually "pops."

Complement the collection with neutral-color accents. Four egg engravings in matching frames and mats add elegance to the wall surrounding the cabinet. An additional print is placed atop the cabinet, along with large and tall items that wouldn't fit within the cabinet.

The overall neutral palette in this room is well-suited to the collection. The taupe leather chair now holds comfy white pillows, one in cotton duck stamped with a green leaf motif.

VERSION THREE: THE DOG THEME

Dog collectibles of every shape, size, and vintage fill the bookcase and find a home atop or next to it. Statues, books, baskets, and dog-motif photo frames fill the case; larger statues and a print in an ornate frame are placed on top.

Unify the look with artwork and textiles. To balance the display, more vintage dog etchings and drawings in antique frames are hung on the wall, and a dark-stained shelf holds an additional dog figure. Dog-theme literature and needlepoint pillows with dog motifs pull the look together.

Ironstone and stoneware of various shapes and sizes create a unified collection because they share a common color: white.

DISPLAY DOS AND DON'TS

When you are ready to create your own artful arrangement, keep the following in mind:

- **Do** use a tried-and-true formula: Starting at the top left corner of the bookcase or shelving unit, trace the letter Z. Place the largest items first at the "points" of the letter (upper left, upper right, vertically down and across the shelves, and then lower left and right). Fill in the remaining spaces with shorter, smaller vertical- and horizontal-oriented accessories. Reverse the zigzag pattern on an adjoining or flanking set of shelves if you are working with a large bookcase wall.
- **Do** stack items for additional height and visual interest; for instance, top a stack of books with a basket or framed piece of artwork.
- **Do** take a step back after you have arranged your collection. Is it too full? Are there areas that still need filling in? Taking a snapshot of the display can help you get a better sense of how it works together. Check the balance of your design; your eyes tend to go toward the voids, or empty spaces, on the shelves.
- **Don't** let overflow find its way onto tables. Keep tabletops clean for contrast.
- **Don't** feel that you have to purchase new items to fill a too empty bookcase. Rethink the objects that you already have and love. Consider arranging and grouping them in new ways to give them unity.
- **Don't** place too small items in a bookcase. They may look great when grouped on a tabletop, but they can become lost when tucked on shelves with larger, more visually dominating elements. For example, a large tole tray on a stand has more visual impact on a shelf than a dozen tiny boxes would.

Displaying Collections

Even if you don't consider yourself a collector, you no doubt have items that you cherish and want to display. Whether you have vintage photographs of ancestors, found items from walks along the beach or in the woods, or toys from your childhood, personalize your home by showcasing what you love.

A beautiful collection of Native American bowls lines the perimeter in this kitchen. This is a great way to display any type of collectible bowl or other dishware.

If you have a collection you love, why not take it one step further? This collection of miniature teapots is thoughtfully arranged in custom teapot-shape shadow boxes. Translate the idea for other collections, perhaps using a spool of thread to hold a thimble collection.

Grouping a collection is a great way to showcase it: These clocks have found a home in an old divided crate.

The corner of this kitchen is filled with a treasure trove of antiques and collectibles. A collection of Red Wing pottery and spongeware resides in the vintage pie safe. Inexpensive whisk brooms create a makeshift valance.

Greenhouse windows in a breakfast room host a collection of birdhouses, bringing a fresh, springlike feel to the space. The birdhouses are grouped with other outdoor collectibles, including watering cans and garden tools.

ARRANGING COLLECTIONS

Follow these guidelines when displaying a collection or group of items on a shelf or a tabletop or in a cabinet.

- **Vary the height.** Incorporate items of different heights, from short to tall. If all your items are of similar height, boost some of them up on pedestals or stacks of books for interest.
- **Ponder proportion.** Besides the height of an item, it is also important to consider its proportion—and how it interacts with other items. An enormous chair in a small room looks awkward and out of place. The same is true of a display space, such as a tabletop.
- **Consider weight.** Due to their size, color, and shape, some items appear heavy to the eye, while others are light. When you arrange your items, pretend you're balancing them on a scale. The visual weight of the pieces should be equal.
- **Be aware of balance.** When items are paired, they lack interest. In an overall symmetrical arrangement, incorporate a small asymmetrical vignette to add some drama.
- **Appeal to your senses.** Items often have implied texture you can see, and actual texture you can touch. Freely mix items with varying textures.
- **Be true to the palette.** Display items that work in the larger scope of the entire room. Are the colors complementary to the wall, the furnishings, and the flooring?

✳ For more tips on decorating with collectibles, visit **HGTV.com/beforeandafterbook**

More Than a
PORCH

This long, narrow enclosed porch is too small to be used as a stand-alone room, but it's a perfect buffer zone between indoors and out. To make this dreary space an appealing entry, outdoor elements are brought inside.

Bring the feeling of the outdoors in. Boldly striped wallpaper hangs like an awning along the sloped ceiling and onto a scalloped-edge plywood window valance. The walls are papered in a faux-stone pattern, and the bench cushions are covered in a black background ivy-trellis pattern. Clunky metal windows hide behind white, wood-slatted blinds that control light levels and provide privacy.

Completing the outdoor theme are botanical prints on the wall, a high-quality outdoor light fixture near the door, a bound sea grass rug, and silk topiaries.

QUICK BENCHES

If you'd like to have a bench under a bank of windows, but don't want to make it from scratch, use prefab kitchen cabinets available in home improvement stores. The cabinet designed to go over a refrigerator is about the right height once it sits on a base. Buy as many as you need to fill the space and create filler strips from board stock the same width as the cabinet frames. You'll need to build a 1- or 2-inch-high base and create a top from plywood. Check that all pieces are held together tightly and firmly attached to the wall, the same as you would if the cabinets were being hung in the kitchen. Choose door hardware that's fairly flat so it doesn't bump people in the back of the legs when they sit on the bench.

BEFORE

AFTER

CREATE AN INDOOR AWNING

Measure the length of the wall or windows to be covered. Use that measurement to make a valance from ¼-inch birch plywood cut 11½ inches wide, with rounded notches cut on the bottom edge to look like scalloped-edge fabric.

Sand and prime the valance sections before putting them in place above the windows. Hold the valance in place with screws on the window frames, so it can be removed at a later date. Then caulk the spaces between boards and the joint between ceiling and valance to give a smooth edge that hides all the joints.

To hang the wallpaper, size the walls and wood valance. That makes it easier to remove wallpaper at a later date. Even if the paper is prepasted, use wallpaper paste to ensure good adhesion to the ceiling.

Hang the wallpaper with the stripes forming one continuous line from the high point of the ceiling down to the edge of the valance. Using a sharp razor blade, cut the wallpaper at the edge of the valance; don't try to wrap it around the bottom. With matching paint and some patience, paint stripes the same width as the wallpaper motif on the valance to complete the look.

Bench Cushion Cover

Creating a custom cushion is easier than you might have imagined. If you cover a long bench, such as this one (which is 14 feet long), making two or three smaller cushions is more manageable than making one. Look for 3-inch-thick foam with good density; squeeze the foam and choose one that's fairly firm rather than one that squishes easily. Cutting the foam to the length and width of the final cushion plus ½ inch all around ensures a tight fit with a firm surface.

You Will Need

Tape measure
3"-thick foam, cut to size of bench
   plus ½" all around
Polyester batting
45"-wide decorator fabric

Scissors
Sewing machine, matching thread
Zipper, the length of the cushion
Premade piping

1. Measure the bench. Purchase 3-inch-thick foam cut to this size plus ½ inch all around. Wrap the foam in polyester batting.

2. Cut the top and bottom fabric to the same length and width as the foam plus 1 inch all around for seam allowances.

3. Cut two 3-inch-wide fabric strips the length of the cushion back. Using a basting stitch, stitch the pieces together lengthwise.

4. Place an upholstery zipper that's slightly shorter than the length of the back facedown over the basted seam. Stitch the two sides of the zipper to the fabric. Pull out the basting stitches.

5. With the zipper in the center of the fabric, trim the piece to 4 inches wide (3-inch cushion depth plus two ½-inch seam allowances).

6. Cut the fabric 4 inches wide along the length of the pattern to wrap around the remaining three sides of the cushion and wrap around the back to the ends of the zipper section. You may need to sew several pieces together.

7. Overlap the strips on the zipper.

8. Stitch the piping to the top and bottom pieces of the cushion, ½ inch from the edge. (Illustration 1) Stitch the zipper section to the back edge of the top and bottom sections, ½ inch from the edge. (Illustration 2)

9. Starting at one end of the zipper section, sew the strip to the top of the cushion; work your way around the cushion. You'll finish at the other end of the zipper section, and you'll be able to remove any extra fabric. Repeat by sewing along the bottom of the cushion.

10. Trim the corners and turn the piece inside out. Insert the batting-wrapped foam into the cushion cover.

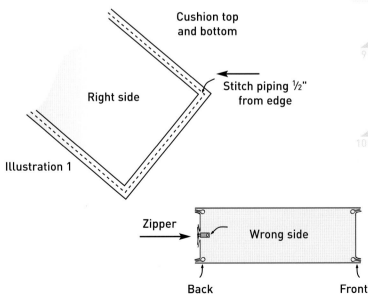

Cushion top and bottom

Right side

Stitch piping ½" from edge

Illustration 1

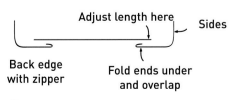

Zipper

Wrong side

Back   Front

Adjust length here   Sides

Back edge with zipper   Fold ends under and overlap

Illustration 2

MORE IDEAS FOR

Porches

Open-air, screened in, or surrounded by glass, a porch says "summer" better than anything else. Because you use a porch for relaxation, entertaining, and casual conversation, it is a natural extension of your home that deserves a style all its own. Consider how the space is most often used, then create the porch of your dreams: Do you need lots of seating and table space for large gatherings or only a couple of chairs for intimate conversation? Could the floor benefit from easy-to-clean rugs or a fun painted treatment? If you don't have a porch, is there a room in your home that could play the role? Regardless of your space, use these examples as a guide.

This back porch is actually an addition. The wide open space allows guests to linger and admire the garden and immaculate yard, including an antique birdhouse.

Screen porches let in fresh air and sunlight and keep out unwanted bugs. Awning-stripe fabrics in springlike colors complement the painted wicker, wood, and metal furnishings.

This rambling sunporch is an ideal place to chat or have a midafternoon snack. The floor is painted in a diamond pattern of white and periwinkle blue; no-sew window treatments carry through the blue and white theme.

If you don't have a porch and long for one, bring in the outdoors with plants, summery fabrics, and a place to lounge. Positioned next to large windows, this daybed is a get-away-from-it-all retreat.

Credits & Resources

PAGES 8–11.
Designer/Stylist: Becky Jerdee. **Photographer:** Bill Hopkins.

PAGES 14–19.
Designer/Stylist: Donna Talley, Ivy Vine Design. **Photographer:** Michael Partenio. **Slipcovers:** Jean Fleming. **Both Versions:** Paint: SW6135 Ecru, Sherwin-Williams (www.sherwinwilliams.com); Window treatments: Country Curtains, (www.countrycurtainscatalog.com); Curtain rods: Home Depot (www.homedepot.com); Parsons chairs: Herb 'n' Country, Great Barrington, MA. **Version One, French:** Sisal rug: Pier 1 Imports, (www.pier1.com); White pitcher: Target (www.target.com). **Version Two, Contemporary:** Faux fur throw, torchieré light, round glass table: Target (www.target.com); Oil painting: Steven Spann (www.stevenspann.com); Sisal rug: Calico Corners (www.calicocorneronline.com).

PAGES 22–25.
Designer/Stylist: Cathy Kramer, Cathy Kramer Design. **Photographer:** Bill Hopkins. **Slipcovers:** Sonja Carmon. **Storage Box Project:** Cathy Kramer, Cathy Kramer Design. Chair fabric: 667042 Melrose Stripe-Amethyst, Waverly (www.waverly.com); Love seat fabric: Silas-10 (floral), 22656-10 (stripe), 11759-10 (piping), Kravet (www.kravet.com). Ottoman fabric: 990104-110 Marguerite Weave, thistle, Kravet (www.kravet.com). Accent pillows: 2001117-10 Pansy Matelasse, amethyst, Kravet (www.kravet.com). Lamps: Luna candlestick lamp with medium square bell shade in silk celadon, Small Genie table lamp in silver with small hourglass shade in silk celadon, Jamie Young (call 888-671-5883 for a retailer near you); Glass jars, acrylic frames: tag (773.697.6300/www.tagltd.com); Beaded photo frames, tall glass candle holder: Pier 1 (www.pier1.com); Banded rug, Colonial Mills (www.colonialmills.com); Carpet: Opening night 7F768 (S), Oyster #00102, 12-foot width, Shaw www.shawfloors.com; Windows: Simonton Windows (www.simontonwindows.com).

PAGES 28–31.
Designer/Stylist: Susan Andrews. **Photographer:** Bob Greenspan. **Decorative Painter:** Tina Blanck. Paint: HC-7, HC-13, HC-16, 2158-20, Benjamin Moore (www.benjaminmoore.com); Lamps: Target (www.target.com); Rug: Pottery Barn (www.potterybarn.com).

PAGES 34–37.
Field Editor: Linda Krinn. **Interior Designer:** Nancy Hilliard. **Photographer:** Ross Chapple. **Armoire Project:** Nancy Hilliard. Window treatments: Sewn by J&L Interiors, designed by Beekeeper's Cottage. Furnishings, fabrics, slipcovers, lighting, and accessories: Beekepeer's Cottage, 43738 Hay Rd., Ashburn, VA 20147 (703-726-9411/www.beekeeperscottage.com).

PAGES 40–43.
Designer/Stylist: Gayle Schadendorf. **Photographer:** Ed Gohlich. **Bench and Ottoman Projects:** Gayle Schadendorf. Fabric (stripe): Sidewalk Stripe, Mint, #666212, Waverly, (www.waverly.com); Fabric (floral): U-Dorable/spring #0006728, Calico Corner Fabrics (www.calicocorneronline.com; Sheer ribbon: Midori Ribbon, (www.midoriribbon.com); Vases, window treatments, curtain rods: Cost Plus World Market (www.costplus.com); Sleeper sofa: Kelly's Furniture, San Diego, CA (858-874-6880); Artwork: David Hebble Photography, Coronado, CA (619-203-6919); Trunk: Target (www.target.com); Faux suede, Field's Fabrics (www.fieldsfabrics.com); Magazine boxes and storage boxes: IKEA (www.ikea.com).

PAGES 48–51.
Designer/Stylist: Donna Talley, Ivy Vine Design. **Photographer:** Michael Partenio. **Refrigerator Bulletin Board and Dishwasher Panel Projects:** Donna Talley, Ivy Vine Design. Knobs: Bruce Hall Corporation (607-547-9961); Paint (cabinets): SW7105, Sherwin-Williams (www.sherwinwilliams); Paint (walls): 8186, Martha Stewart (www.marthastewart.com); Flooring: SwiftLock laminate, Armstrong (www.armstrong.com); Lamps, bowl, pitcher, dishtowel: Target (www.target.com); Wood stool: A.C. Moore (www.acmoore.com).

PAGES 54–57.
Designer/Stylist: Deborah Hastings. **Photographer:** Sylvia Martin. **Curtain Project:** Deborah Hastings. Paint (cabinets and walls): Beachcomber 20 YY 58/082, Glidden (www.glidden.com); Paint (trim): Swiss Coffee 2012, ICI Paints (www.glidden.com); Countertop: Bronze Legacy 4656-60, Wilson Art (www.wilsonart.com).

PAGES 60–63.
Designer/Stylist: Cathy Kramer, Cathy Kramer Design. **Photographer:** Kent Clawson. **Cabinet Painting:** Patty Mohr Kramer. Base Coat (walls): #2012 Swiss Coffee, Glidden (www.glidden.com); Base Coat (yellow cabinets): Yellowhammer, Ralph Lauren (www.ralphlauren.com); Base Coat (red cabinets): Barn Red Ralph Lauren; Toile wallpaper: Classics Lifestyles, #564300, Wavelry (www.waverly.com); Toile fabric: Classic Lifestyles book, Country Life fabric, #659430, Waverly; Countertop: Manitoba Maple, #7911-60, Wilsonart (www.wilsonart.com); Faucet: #K-690, Vinnata Kitchen Sink Faucet with Pull-Down Spray, Brushed Nickel, Kohler (www.kohler.com); Hardware: #BP9365-G10 Bin Pulls, #BP1586-G10 Knobs, Amerock (www.amerock.com); Woven shade: Tahiti, Straw Hut #WWTA245A96F, Hunter Douglas (www.hunterdouglas.com); Appliances: G.E. (www.ge.com).

PAGES 66–69.
Designer/Stylist: Deborah Hastings. **Photographer:** Sylvia Martin. Wallpaper: Terra Verde (walls) and Sunny Tuscany (ceiling), Seabrook (www.seabrookwallcoverings.com).

PAGES 72–75.
Designer/Stylist: Diane Carroll. **Photographer:** Colleen Duffley. **Beaded-Board Project:** Diane Carroll. Oven/range: JennAir (www.jennair.com); Dishwasher: Asko (www.askousa.com); Toaster, coffee maker: Michael Graves, Target (www.target.com); Stand mixer: KitchenAid (www.kitchenaid.com); Artwork: Scott Carroll, through Kristy Stubbs French Gallery (214-871-9311/mail@stubbsgallery.com); Butcher-block countertops: John Boos and Co. (www.homedepot.com). Beaded-board panel kit: Home Depot (www.homedepot.com).

PAGES 78–81.
Designer/Stylist: Jeni Hilpipre. **Photographer:** Tim Murphy/Foto Imagery. Cake stand on table: Bimboveloce, Chiasso (www.chiasso.com); Dining chairs: Design Within Reach (www.dwr.com); Wineglass area rug: Pottery Barn (www.potterybarn.com); Glass container for fish: Crate and Barrel (www.crateandbarrel.com); Fabric: Duralee Fabrics, Ltd. (www.duralee.com).

PAGES 84–87.
Designers/Stylists: Linda Krinn. **Interior Designer:** Nancy Hilliard. **Photographer:** Ross Chapple. **Slipcover information:** Donna Talley, Ivy Vine Design, and Jean Fleming. Furnishings, fabrics, slipcovers, lighting, and accessories: Beekepeer's Cottage, 43738 Hay Rd., Ashburn, VA 20147 (703-726-9411/www.beekeeperscottage.com).

PAGES 90–93.
Designer/Stylist: Joetta Moulden (www.shelterstyle.com; info@shelterstyle.com).
Photographer: Janet Lenzen.

PAGES 96–99.
Designer/Stylist: Joetta Moulden (www.shelterstyle.com; info@shelterstyle.com).
Photographer: Janet Lenzen. Paint: #1301, Benjamin Moore
(www.benjaminmoore.com).

PAGES 104–107.
Designer/Stylist: Deborah Hastings. **Photographer:** Sylvia Martin. **Headboard
Project:** Deborah Hastings. Paint: Mexican Springs 1441 (walls), Swiss Coffee
2012 (trim), ICI Paints (www.glidden.com); Chair: Pier 1 Imports
(www.pier1.com); Bedding: Garnet Hill (www.garnethill.com).

PAGES 110–113.
Designer/Stylist: Deborah Hastings. **Photographer:** Sylvia Martin. Wallpaper: Tropical
Breezes (walls) and Cyprus Garden (ceiling), Seabrook (www.seabrookwallcoverings.com);
Quilt: Pottery Barn (www.potterybarn.com).

PAGES 116–119.
Designer/Stylist: Becky Jerdee. **Photographer:** Bill Hopkins. **Shutter Project:**
David Underwood. Closet storage: Qbits Modular Furniture System by Sauder
and Lynette Jennings (www.sauder.com).

PAGES 122–125.
Designer/Stylist: Gayle Schadendorf. **Photographer:** Ed Gohlich. **Pillow,
Nightstand Top, and Chandelier Projects:** Gayle Schadendorf. Ribbon: Offray.
Paint: SW6521, Sherwin-Williams (www.sherwinwilliams.com); Bed coverlet,
blue chenille throw, night stand: Ross Stores (www.rossstores.com); Hanging
lamp: IKEA (www.ikeausa.com).

PAGES 128–131.
Designer/Stylist: Stacy Kunstel. **Photographer:** Paul Whicheloe/Anyway
Productions. Crewel fabric, antique linens, tassels, alarm clock, mirror,
lamp: Red Chair Antiques & Collectibles, Peterborough, NH (603-924-5953);
Nightstand, wall platter, candle sconces, curtain rod: Yankee Candle Company
(www.yankeecandle.com); Iron planters: Friend of a Gardner, Peterborough, NH
(603-924-9278); Paint (wall): 4C4-3, Behr (www.behr.com); Paint (wall trim and
chest): Magnolia White, Martha Stewart (www.marthastewart.com).

PAGES 134–137.
Designer/Stylist: Cathy Kramer, Cathy Kramer Design. **Photographer:** Andy
Lyons. **Dresser Project:** Cathy Kramer, Cathy Kramer Design. **Decorative Painter:**
Patty Mohr Kramer. **Duvet Cover:** Sonja Carmon. **Loft Bed:** Designed by Phillip
Crum (978-475-4991). Chest: Maple Shaker Mule Chest, CCM511, Woodcraft
Industries (www.woodcraftindustries.com); Blinds: Zig-Zag blind in Walnut,
Kirsch (www.kirsch.com); Paint (magnetic): Magic Wall magnetic paint, Kling
Magnetics (www.kling.com); Paint: 6607 (walls), 6635 (dressers), Sherwin
Williams (www.sherwinwilliams.com); Chair: Conrad in #100271 Jade/Raisin,
Mitchell Gold (www.mitchellgold.com); Ottomans: Link in #11245 Jamboree/Raisin,
Mitchell Gold (www.mitchellgold.com); Faux Suede: Kanto Italiano in #3714 Red
Ultra Suede, #3705 Brown, #3701 Tan, Synergized Fabrics, Inc. (617-889-4150);
Closet storage: Closits Modular Storage System by Sauder and Lynette
Jennings and Qbits Modular Furniture System by Sauder and Lynette Jennings
(www.sauder.com); Rickrack: Wrights (www.wrights.com)

PAGES 140–145.
Designer/Stylist: Donna Talley, Ivy Vine Design. **Photographer:** Michael
Partenio. **Roman Shade Project Instructions:** Deborah Hastings. **Both Rooms:**
Photographs: Target (www.target.com); **Bedroom:** Paint: SW6127, Sherwin Williams
(www.sherwinwilliams.com); Bed, nightstand: Retro Ve Collection, Thomasville
Furniture (www.thomasville.com); Carpet: LA747 Castlebury in 5757 Honey,
Laura Ashley at Lowe's (www.lowes.com); Lamp (dresser): Eddie Bauer Home
(www.eddiebaurehome.com); Lamp (nightstand), suede pillows (bed): Linens 'n
Things (www.lnt.com); Window treatments: Sailcloth panels in Natural #5053, Tortoise
Shell Roman Shades #48515, Country Curtains (www.countrycurtainscatalog.com);
Picture Target (www.target.com); Leather pillow (chair): Pottery Barn
(www.potterybarn.com); Wicker chair: Pier 1 (www.pier1.com). **Bathroom:** Paint:
SW6129, Sherwin Williams (www.sherwinwilliams.com); Light fixture: Hampton
Bay at Home Depot (www.homedepot.com); Flooring: Rialto 4x4 ceramic tile,
Lowe's (www.lowes.com); Window treatments: Sailcloth Roman Shade in Natural
#485e, Country Curtains (www.countrycurtainscatalog.com); Towel bars: Linens
'n Things (www.lnt.com).

PAGES 150–153.
Designer/Stylist: Joetta Moulden (www.shelterstyle.com; info@shelterstyle.com).
Interior Design: John Kidd & Associates. **Photographer:** Hal Lott. **Chest Project:**
Joetta Moulden. All brass hardware, plumbing, and lighting fixtures: The
Renovator's Supply (www.rensup.com). Fabrics: Classic Ticking in Khaki, Polka,
Glosheen Lining in White, Waverly (www.waverly.com); Wallpaper: Boxer in
Antique Linen, Waverly (www.waverly.com).

PAGES 156–159.
Designer/Stylist: Susan Andrews. **Photographer:** Bob Greenspan. **Dresser
Project:** Susan Andrews. **Contractor:** Greg Heiman, Heiman Development,
Kansas City, MO (816-942-0000). Paint: 90GG49/159 (wall), 90YY48/255 (accent
on mirror), Glidden (www.glidden.com); Faucet: HansGrohe, Axor Phillipe Starck
design (www.hansgrohe.com); Sink, toilet: Kohler (www.kohler.com); Lamps:
Home Depot (www.homedepot.com); Tile (floor): Metro Ceramincs Grey, Home
Depot (www.homedepot.com); Tile (wall): 12x12 Cream, Lowe's (www.lowes.com).

PAGES 162–165.
Designer/Stylist: Donna Talley, Ivy Vine Design. **Photographer:** Michael Partenio.
Display Shelf Project: Donna Talley, Ivy Vine Design. Roman shade: Created by
Val Papero, The Shade Place. Valance: Created by Susan Cuda, Designer's
Choice. Fabric: Calico Corners (www.calicocorneronline.com); Wallpaper:
Thibault (purchased at Signature Interiors, Saratoga Springs, NY,
saratogasignature.com).

PAGES 168–171.
Designer/Stylist: Deborah Hastings. **Photographer:** Sylvia Martin. **Mirror
Project:** Deborah Hastings. Wallpaper: Remembered Places, Seabrook
(www.seabrookwallcoverings.com).

PAGES 174–177.
Designer/Stylist: Donna Talley, Ivy Vine Design. **Photographer:** Tria Giovan. **Both
Versions:** Window treatments: Country Curtains (www.countrycurtains.com).

Credits & Resources

PAGES 182–185.
Designer/Stylist: Cathy Kramer, Cathy Kramer Design. **Photographer:** Bill Hopkins. **Chair Upholstery:** Sonja Carmon. Wallpaper: Village PaperIllusion Color Multi #5805265, FSC Wallcoverings (www.villagehome.com); Lights: Bendable rail system, Tiella (www.tiella.com); Hearth: Thermo-Rite, ultraview, satin-nickel finish, clear glass, HearthCraft (www.hearthcraft.com); Hardware: Handles #19205 WN, Amerock Corporation (www.amerock.com); Pillows: Pier 1 (www.pier1.com); Faux suede fabric: Kanto Italiano #3733 Black Ultra Suede (chair), #3702 Camel (chair), #3730 Gray (built-in seating), Synergized Fabrics (617-889-4150); Upholstery tacks: #1585 Brass 54, Pewter Zinc finish, Turner and Seymour (www.turnerseymour.com); Architectural trims: Georgia-Pacific Corp. (www.gp.com); Rug: Sausalito #2280 in Ebony #300, Capel, Inc. (www.capelrugs.com); Firewood holder: Umbra (www.umbra.com); Floor: Bruce Hardwood Floors, 4¼" Bruce Birchall Plank in Adobe, Armstrong (www.bruce.com/www.armstrong.com).

PAGES 188–191.
Designer/Stylist: Cathy Kramer, Cathy Kramer Design. **Photographer:** Kent Clawson. **Mirror Project:** Cathy Kramer, Cathy Kramer Design. Storage Units and Furniture: Closits Modular Storage System by Sauder and Lynette Jennings and Qbits Modular Furniture System by Sauder and Lynette Jennings (www.sauder.com); Blinds: Ty Reed in Umber, Kirsch (www.kirsch.com); Rugs: 2x6 runner in wide stripe black and taupe, Colonial Mills (www.colonialmills.com); Mirror brackets: #MP6408 in Chrome Victorian, Advance Glass (www.advanceglasscreations.com); Pillows and accessories: Pier 1 (www.pier1.com).

PAGES 194–197.
Designer/Stylist: Stacy Kunstel. **Photographer:** Paul Whicheloe, Anyway Productions. **Pillow Project:** Wendy Hiraoka, Hiraoka Home, Honolulu, HI (www.hiraokahome.com). **Window Seat Project:** Steve Copplestone, Copplestone Woodcrafts, 79 Winter Harbor, Wolfeboro, NH 03894 (603-569-9290). Candlestick table, chair, crystal lamp: American Home Gallery, Wolfeboro, NH (603-569-8989); Merino wool throw: Out of the Blue, Wolfeboro, NH (603-569-8644); Paint (walls): Jackson Antique, California Paints (www.californiapaints.com); Paint (floor): Thundercloud, Glidden (www.glidden.com); Mirror: Ethan Allen (www.ethanallen.com).

PAGES 200–203.
Designer/Stylist: Joetta Moulden (www.shelterstyle.com; info@shelterstyle.com). **Photographer:** Fran Brennan. **Cabinet:** Interior painting by Sammie Cockrell, Faux FX, 11418 Lakeside Place Dr., Houston, TX 77077 (sjcockrell@houston.rr.com). Framing: Arden's Picture Framing, 1631 West Alabama, Houston, TX 77006 (713-522-5281). Custom dog portraits, tramp art frame, sap buckets, pails, cake pedestals, pitchers: Shelter Style (www.shelterstyle.com).

PAGES 206–209.
Designer/Stylist: Deborah Hastings. **Photographer:** Sylvia Martin. **Cushion Project:** Deborah Hastings. Wallpaper: The Art of Cheri Blum (walls), Tropical Breezes (ceiling), Seabrook (www.seabrookwallcoverings.com).

Index

Index